CROSSCURRENTS *Modern Critiques*

CROSSCURRENTS *Modern Critiques*

Harry T. Moore, *General Editor*

Joseph Prescott

Exploring James Joyce

WITH A PREFACE BY

Harry T. Moore

Carbondale

SOUTHERN ILLINOIS UNIVERSITY PRESS

To My Mother
and the Memory of My Father

2954

A SILLY LITTLE WORD-GAME known as "Tom Swifties" was so popular in the United States in the 1960s that publishers actually made millions of dollars with "Tom Swifties" books. Most players of the game would have been startled to learn that an Irish writer about whom they probably knew very little had been a "Tom Swifties" player long before. James Joyce, that inveterate and elaborate punster, had anticipated the game by some forty years. Consider this passage from the famous nighttown scene (Chapter 15) of Ulysses (1922):

> [Women whisper eagerly.]
> A MILLIONAIRESS
> [richly] Isn't he simply wonderful?
> A NOBLEWOMAN
> [nobly] All that man has seen!
> A FEMINIST
> [masculinely] And done!

There are other examples. Joyce would probably have been drily amused at the "Tom Swifties" game, though he would have realized that it wouldn't necessarily bring him any more readers. Yet the avid player of the game could be someone on his way to reading Ulysses and Finnegans Wake. Certainly he would have to bring much more to the understanding of Joyce, much more than most "Tom Swifties" players would be endowed with: some literary sensibility, at least a small acquaintance with culture, and at least a small acquaintance with several languages beyond English. But the "Tom Swifties" adept would have some appreciation of an important part of Joyce: the word play. Quite appropriately, Joseph Prescott calls the first chapter of the present book "James Joyce: A Study in Words." And his entire volume is essentially that, for his exploration of Joyce is largely an exploration of his texts.

Mr. Prescott in this study is concerned chiefly with the two Dedalus books, A Portrait of the Artist and Ulysses; one chapter deals specifically with the surviving parts of the Ur-Portrait, Stephen Hero. But most of the present volume concerns Ulysses. In working with his material, Mr. Prescott has over the years consulted the most important sources available to him. He has of course made use of all the published texts in English except the latest Modern Library Edition, which appeared too late to be considered in this volume (the new Modern Library Edition came as a surprise to people working in the field, just another imperfect text of Joyce's novel). Mr. Prescott has also scrutinized manuscripts, including those now at the Rosenbach Foundation and the Lockwood Memorial Library of the University of Buffalo. Further, he has investigated the sets of proof sheets which are located at the University of Texas Library and at the Houghton Library of Harvard University.

In examining these materials and organizing the discoveries he has made in them, Mr. Prescott has given us an important picture of an artist at work. Everyone has always known that Joyce was a deliberate and careful writer; to what extent, Mr. Prescott shows us exactly. In the passage quoted earlier from Joyce, for example, the millionairess says "richly," "Isn't he wonderful?" Mr. Prescott notes on p. 108 that the qualifying adverb didn't come to Joyce at once. An abbreviation in the manuscript suggests that he had first intended to write "enthusiastically," then took that out and put in "adoringly." But he deleted that and inserted "the highly appropriate 'richly,' which consists with the millionairess as 'nobly' does with the noblewoman and 'masculinely' with the feminist."

This is much labor over a single little word, but it does improve the passage. Joyce made such changes again and again throughout his work, as the many examples in this book indicate. And, as Mr. Prescott says, Joyce in his revisions intensifies what he is writing about. "Intensifies" is the proper word, for that is what Joyce does in almost every case.

Sometimes, however, he nods, and Mr. Prescott, who as scholar and critic doesn't nod, notes when this happens with Joyce, as in the two "confusions" mentioned on p. 110. There are other slips of this kind elsewhere, duly recorded; they usually result from a change that requires another change to balance it, as in the first example noted on p. 110, in the passage in which Joyce substituted "he" for "they" in the second of three sentences quoted; the change in number means that, in the third sentence, "he said" should have become "Lenihan said." Again this is a small point, but there is a confusion in the text; no reader, especially of a difficult text, should be forced by such ambiguities to figure out who the speaker or actor is, especially when there is no recognizable clue. Mr. Prescott knows that in this case the speaker is Lenihan; he knows this because he has consulted the earlier, unchanged version, to which most readers don't have access.

Joyce was writing good, if not great, prose. But writing even good prose is, as everyone should know, an arduous task. And one of the great difficulties for the meticulous craftsman is making changes that require other changes, for in the effort to heighten one passage, the author doesn't always see how the alteration affects another passage. If he does notice, and changes the second passage also, it in turn may create the necessity for still other changes. The process of keeping all these details straight is a bit like the situation used in silent films when the comedian (Harry Langdon, say) was left alone in a room and a door would open. He would close it, and another door in the room would open. When he shut that one, the first would swing open again. The two doors were just far enough apart so that he couldn't hold the knobs of both at once; the shutting of one door always meant the opening of the other. Writing flawless prose means, among other things, that the author must, in closing one door, somehow also manage to shut the other one that is tantalizingly out of reach.

Some readers might ask, and do ask, why all this is so important. These are not necessarily nonliterary readers, either, but are often compulsive booklovers or trained critics, both types sophisticated beyond the point of those outraged puritans who used to feel that Joyce should be suppressed as a writer of pornography or blasphemy, or of both. Censors of that type have been badly defeated, for the Woolsey-Hand decisions in the American Courts in 1933–34 have made possible the publication of Ulysses elsewhere in the English-speaking world except, it seems, in Joyce's native country. The criticisms that Joyce is too obscure have also tended to disappear, largely because of the various explications, guides, and "keys," the interpretations of which are under continual dispute. But most serious readers now agree, or have discovered, that Joyce's obscurity can be pierced; not all the way, perhaps, but most of the way. (Thornton Wilder has said that he'd like to write a whole book discussing a single passage of Finnegans Wake; he has also said that he could never write such a book because to do so would put him in the position of someone explaining a joke.)

If criticism of Joyce on the score of obscenity, blasphemy, and obscurity has lessened or almost vanished, the one objection mentioned earlier as being raised by many readers has persisted: the super-Flaubertian fussiness over a single word or phrase. This criticism has been accompanied by another, closely associated with it, to the effect that Joyce lacks spontaneity. Even some of his admirers feel that his concern over words is carried at times to perhaps unnecessary extremes. In the first chapter of the present book, for instance, just after he points out how "the fusion of style with subject has given us some of the most successful of Joyce's chapters," Joseph Prescott admits that "on the other hand, Joyce in some of his tours de force falls flat. The section of parodies describing the scene at the hospital, for example, is a waste of effort. And the scene at Boom's house after the delirium of nighttown, presented in the form of an examination paper! This sort of writing is full of the boredom which poisons the pleasure of the reader in other parts of Ulysses." These are strong statements, which Mr. Prescott first published in 1939; apparently all his subsequent linguistic tracings across the text of Ulysses haven't induced in him a change of mind which would lead him to cancel the passage in the present reprinting, although many other commentators like those two episodes, especially the hospital scene.

As I write this preface, the latest full-bodied study of Joyce is the long essay in J. I. M. Stewart's Eight Modern Writers. Mr. Stewart finds much good in Joyce, but notes that it is "hard not to conclude that the elaborative method at times becomes merely mechanical, something that goes on operating by rote rather than upon specific artistic consideration." This is a variant of the criticism I mentioned earlier as having endured in relation to Joyce; and a good many other commentators beyond Messrs. Stewart and Prescott could be called in to substantiate the point that the "merely mechanical," the "examination paper" style, and "the boredom which poisons the reader in other parts of Ulysses" are elements which most critics note.

But what of it? Although this aspect of Joyce's writing is consistently mentioned, it is not usually held to be a major fault. This is certainly true of J. I. M. Stewart's total view of Joyce, and here we have Mr. Prescott's entire book to show that the matter is incidental with him. Mr. Stewart quotes Edmund Wilson's estimate of Joyce as "the great poet of a new phase of the human consciousness," and goes on to say, "Yet however we judge Ulysses at the level of high philosophical consideration we are likely to return to it again and again as fiction. We shall revisit it—Mr. Wilson has said—as we revisit a city, a city animated by a complex inexhaustible life."

Joseph Prescott's book will help us make those return trips to Joyce's Dublin. And in the process it will illustrate many of the problems of imaginative writing. Imaginative writing of a certain kind, that is—not the spontaneous.

Spontaneity often characterizes great writing, if not the greatest; the men who create in this fashion may never blot out a line and may cause a more deliberate craftsman to wish that they had blotted a thousand, but their work remains, often "out-topping knowledge." Yet the value of the non-spontaneous writer is often great also, and in our time Joyce is a notable example of the type. He works not only by excision but also, and more frequently, by augmentation. In going over his text, he qualifies and expands and, to use the word quoted earlier, "intensifies." Mr. Prescott quotes Stendhal's definition of style, which justifies the method of addition ("ajouter," to add). How successfully Joyce did this, most of the time, Mr. Prescott shows us more thoroughly than anyone else has, and this alone makes his book one of the significant textual explorations of a modern author. There is much else in his volume, all of it a welcome enrichment of studies of the Dedalus books. The title, which justifiably uses the word "exploring," was not that of the modest Mr. Prescott: we added ("avons ajouté") that.

HARRY T. MOORE

Southern Illinois University
September 21, 1963

ACKNOWLEDGMENTS

"James Joyce: A Study in Words" appeared in *PMLA*, LIV (March 1939), 304–15, and was reprinted in part by W. E. Morris and C. A. Nault, Jr., eds., *Portraits of an Artist: A Casebook on James Joyce's "A Portrait of the Artist as a Young Man"* (New York: Odyssey Press [1962]). Readers of Dutch will find remarkable coincidences between this essay and Anthony Bosman's *De Revolutie van het Woord* (Bussum: Uitgeverij F. G. Kroonder, 1947).

"*Stephen Hero*," in somewhat abbreviated form, was read at the annual meeting of the Modern Language Association, in Boston, on December 29, 1952. A documented version appeared as "James Joyce's *Stephen Hero*" in the *Journal of English and Germanic Philology*, LIII (April 1954), 214–23, and in *Letterature Moderne* (Bologna), VI (November–December 1956), 679–88; an undocumented version, in *The Bell* (Dublin), XIX (November 1954), 27–35, and in the *Diliman Review* (Quezon City), VII (October 1959), 373–85; a selectively documented version, in T. E. Connolly, ed., *Joyce's "Portrait": Criticisms and Critiques* (New York: Appleton-Century-Crofts [1962]). A Spanish translation by Jaime Rest appeared in *Sur* (Buenos Aires), no. 250 (January–February 1958), pp. 39–50, and *Armas y Letras* (Monterrey, N.L., Mexico), Second Series, I (October–December 1958), 64–76; a French translation, tr. anon., in *Configuration critique de James Joyce*, ed. Joseph Prescott (Paris: M. J. Minard, 1959–60), I, 48–66 (also published as *La Revue des lettres modernes* [Paris], VI [Autumn 1959], 288–306); and a Hebrew translation by Abraham Yavin, in *Moznaim* (Tel Aviv), XIV (January 1962), 137–43. In 1960 a tape-recording by the author was added to the library of World Tapes for Education.

"Homer's *Odyssey* and Joyce's *Ulysses*" appeared in *Modern Language Quarterly*, III (September 1942), 427–44.

"Local Allusions in *Ulysses*" was read at the annual meeting of the Michigan Academy of Science, Arts and Letters, in Detroit, on April 18, 1953; published as "Local Allusions in Joyce's *Ulysses*" in *PMLA*, LXVIII (December 1953), 1223–28, and reprinted in *Letterature Moderne*, XII (October–December 1962), 613–18.

"The Characterization of Stephen Dedalus in *Ulysses*" appeared in *Letterature Moderne*, IX (March–April 1959), 145–63. An abbreviated version was read at the annual meeting of the Modern Language Association of America, at the University of Wisconsin, on September 9, 1957. The writing of the paper and the two which follow was made possible, in part, by a sabbatical leave of absence from Wayne State University and a grant-in-aid from the Modern Language Association of America. Joyce's revisions in the three papers are quoted by permission of the James Joyce Estate.

"The Characterization of Molly Bloom," in an abbreviated version, was read at the Fourth Triennial Conference of the International Association of University Professors of English, at the University of Lausanne, on August 28, 1959. The full text appeared in Marvin Magalaner, ed., *A James Joyce Miscellany: Third Series* (Carbondale: Southern Illinois University Press [1962]).

"Stylistic Realism in *Ulysses*," in an abbreviated version, was read at the Seventh Triennial Congress of the International Federation for Modern Languages and Literatures, at the University of Heidelberg, on August 27, 1957. The full text appeared as "Stylistic Realism in Joyce's *Ulysses*" in Marvin Magalaner, ed., *A James Joyce Miscellany: Second Series* (Carbondale: Southern Illinois University Press, 1959).

CONTENTS

Exploring James Joyce

1 JAMES JOYCE:
A STUDY IN WORDS

In the beginning was the Word . . .

THE WRITINGS OF JOYCE show a progression from an early interest in words through a mature use of them to the excessive fondness of old age. In spite of variation from one work to another, the development is not always consistent and steady; sometimes there is a reversion to a former phase, sometimes an advance into a future phase. The direction, however, is unmistakable.

Joyce's writings give themselves readily to such analysis, because Stephen Dedalus, "the unnamed narrator of the first three studies in *Dubliners,*" [1] the chief character in *A Portrait of the Artist as a Young Man,* [2] and one of the chief characters in *Ulysses,* [3] is, to a large extent, James Joyce recollected in tranquillity. The danger of indiscriminately identifying even an autobiographical character with its creator is obvious. Usually the author and the character, although two aspects of the same personality, are still two aspects. In words, however, it is not only unwarrantable to distinguish the experiences of the two, it is impossible. Joyce has transformed his life into his art, and, since far and away the most revered thing in his life is the Word, he has put into his art not only his use of words but also his experiences with them and his speculations on these experiences.

In early childhood, when Stephen was being taught the law of the apology, words already formed patterns in his mind.

His mother said:

—O, Stephen will apologise.

Dante said:

—O, if not, the eagles will come and pull out his eyes.—

> Pull out his eyes,
> Apologise,
> Apologise,
> Pull out his eyes.

> Apologise,
> Pull out his eyes,
> Pull out his eyes,
> Apologise.[4]

Stephen's reaction is primarily to sound. This is probably true for most of us. Words begin as sounds and end as symbols. While we are growing into articulation, gradually the representative quality of words supersedes in importance their significance as sound. We cease to trouble ourselves about their success as echoes, and speak, as Seán O'Faoláin says, "not so much in words as by means of words." [5] But this boy continued to be sensitive to their sound, to find in them experiences that shed light on their accepted, dictionary meaning, and to enrich their meaning with the color of his own personality.

At first they stir his memory: "That was a belt round his pocket. And belt was also to give a fellow a belt." [6] A boy at Clongowes is called the prefect's suck, and Stephen ponders:

> Suck was a queer word . . . But the sound was ugly. Once he had washed his hands in the lavatory of the Wicklow Hotel and his father had pulled the stopper up by the chain after and the dirty water went down through the hole in the basin. And when it had all gone down slowly the hole in the basin had made a sound like that: suck. Only louder.[7]

And a little later, baffled by the equivocal attitude of his schoolfellows to kissing one's mother, Stephen remembers: "His mother put her lips on his cheek; her lips were soft and they wetted his cheek; and they made a tiny little noise: kiss." [8]

The sounds of words fascinate the future artist before they breed in him emotions. The prefect of studies is called Dolan, and to Stephen, fresh from a "hot burning stinging tingling" encounter with him, "it was like the name of a woman who washed clothes." [9]

As the boy grows older, words come to fill him with strange sensations. The age of the narrator in the first stories of *Dubliners* is not clear, so that one cannot correlate exactly his reactions there with those in the *Portrait*, but the same preoccupation is recorded:

> Every night as I gazed up at the window I said softly to myself the word paralysis. It had always sounded strangely in my ears, like the word gnomon in the Euclid and the word simony in the Catechism. [10]

Similar thoughts and feelings move the boy throughout his adolescence. It is noteworthy, however, that his artistic yearnings are almost completely submerged during one phase of his religious experience. In all the section of the *Portrait* describing Stephen during the retreat, there is only a single remark on a single word, [11] and that comes so near the beginning of the retreat that it seems to be no more than an isolated instance of perseveration. The incubus of sin crushes every impulse of the artist, stifling, shrivelling. "His soul traversed a period of desolation in which the sacraments themselves seemed to have turned into dried up sources." [12] Only after the deflation of his emotional religiosity, induced in him by the retreat, does Stephen the "fearful jesuit," [13] as he was later to be called, give way to Dedalus the artist. After a violent swing toward faith, there is an equally violent rebound in the direction of disbelief, and Stephen passes "beyond the challenge of the sentries who had stood as guardians of his boyhood and had sought to keep him among them that he might be subject to them and serve their ends." [14]

With his entry into the university Stephen gives full rein to his artistic inclinations. He plays on words as on

the strings of a delicate instrument, he listens intently
for all the overtones, he lives almost exclusively in a world
of word-sensations.

> He drew forth a phrase from his treasure and spoke it
> softly to himself:
>   —A day of dappled seaborne clouds.—
> The phrase and the day and the scene harmonised in a
> chord. Words. Was it their colours? He allowed them to
> glow and fade, hue after hue: sunrise gold, the russet and
> green of apple orchards, azure of waves, the greyfringed
> fleece of clouds. No, it was not their colours: it was the
> poise and balance of the period itself. Did he then love
> the rhythmic rise and fall of words better than their
> associations of legend and colour? Or was it that, being as
> weak of sight as he was shy of mind, he drew less pleasure
> from the reflection of the glowing sensible world through
> the prism of a language manycoloured and richly storied
> than from the contemplation of an inner world of indi-
> vidual emotions mirrored perfectly in a lucid supple
> periodic prose.[15]

The young artist is groping for the precise source of the
power which words wield over him, but it eludes him.
He can only foreknow as matter of fact that at various
stages of his morning walks across the city the spirits of
Hauptmann and Newman and Cavalcanti and Ibsen will
rise in his soul, each with emotions after its kind.

And now we come to a new phase in Stephen's development. Gradually a mysterious unrest has seeped into his
soul, poisoning his pleasure with disillusion. Words became "emptied of instantaneous sense until every mean
shop legend bound his mind like the words of a spell and
his soul shrivelled up sighing with age as he walked on in
a lane of dead language." [16] Slowly and vaguely the young
Dedalus has become aware of an insufficiency in the language. Accepted forms of expression no longer represent
life for him fully. And the feeling is heightened by the
fact that Stephen's education in his most formative years
had been steeped in a forgotten past.

. . . it wounded him to think he would never be but a shy guest at the feast of the world's culture and that the monkish learning in terms of which he was striving to forge out an esthetic philosophy, was held no higher by the age he lived in than the subtle and curious jargons of heraldry and falconry.[17]

Again the single word takes hold of him when he discusses with the English dean of studies the use of *tundish*. The young Irishman envies his instructor for having the tradition of English as a heritage while for himself it is only an acquisition. "His language, so familiar and so foreign," Stephen considers, "will always be for me an acquired speech. I have not made or accepted the words. My voice holds them at bay. My soul frets in the shadow of his language.—"[18]

Allowing for the adolescent tragedy with which the young man laments his fate, it is evident that Stephen, Joyce, did experience early dissatisfaction with accepted forms of speech. He himself probably never dreamt to what lengths that unrest would go. Nor could he have foreseen that he was himself to go through a process of growth in the language, of creation, and ultimately of dissolution. In the *Portrait* he is still moving in a world of conventional language. His interest in its words revolves chiefly about their onomatopoeic associations and their effect upon his spirit. He is now, too, pondering the notion of an esthetic, groping toward the "system" that is to inform his art with a rigidity which finally undoes it. Closely allied to his speculations about words, Joyce's theory of art dominates his use of them in his best work, *Ulysses*.

> . . . *and the Word was with God* . . .

The *Portrait* describes Joyce's linguistic childhood, in which he is gathering strength for *Ulysses*, the production of his manhood. Now Joyce has got, created anew, the Word "with Jehovah" (and is beginning to raise Cain with the language).

In *Ulysses*, the epic of almost as many things as it has critics, Joyce is no longer fumbling. He has put into applied form the results of the dissatisfaction, the speculations, and the experiments with words which he went through during his nonage. The variety and the ubiquity of the application are unparalleled, and it is difficult to approach the work from any one point of view without becoming involved in a number of others. Unlike the *Portrait, Ulysses* does not present a neat, chronologically ordered development in words. The discussion, therefore, will break up and travel along various routes, finally to meet at a point beyond *Ulysses*, in *Work in Progress*.[19]

The first impression in *Ulysses*, no less than in Joyce's former work, is his extreme care in the use of words. The more common variety of this precision has already appeared in his earlier writing. But in *Ulysses* exactness becomes an obsession. Thus, Bloom, anticipating his bath, "foresaw his pale body reclined in it at full, naked, in a womb of warmth, oiled by scented melting soap, softly laved." [20] For liquidity and warmth and perfume and softness the English language could not have supplied a better word with which to end the sentence. The consideration that *laved* is not in common use, Joyce ignores.

Joyce's novelty resolves itself largely into two types, renovation and innovation. The former consists principally of a trick of usage which I shall call Elizabethanism. In Elizabethan literature, often a word of no lustre today is invested with a peculiar vitality, owing to the immediacy of the word in its older application. For us "bombastic circumlocution" is an abstract statement about highflown redundancy. But Othello's "bombast circumstance" [21] still enjoyed the freshness of a metaphor, and the "circumstance" became concrete by comparison with the material which went into cotton padding. Joyce, likewise, imposes on words of common currency a fresh lustre, usually the brilliance of their first years. By Elizabethanism, however, I mean no more, at present, than Joyce's use of words in such a sense or context as to throw upon them a stronger light than they ordinarily enjoy.

Of this practice I find an example as far back as Joyce's first volume of prose. In *Dubliners* (p. 151) he writes: "Imminent little drops of rain hung at the brim of his hat," and, unobtrusively pushing a word back to an earlier, more concrete meaning, Joyce heightens its effectiveness. His usual practice is to *reincarnate* a word which today has become so abstract that it is applied almost exclusively to mental experiences—to give it body again.

Another instance occurs in the use of a word so common today that even the trite hesitate before it. In one of the cloacal scenes of *Ulysses*, Bloom kicks open "the crazy door of the jakes." [22] Again, on the way to Glasnevin the wheels of the funeral carriage "rattled rolling over the cobbled causeway and the crazy glasses shook rattling in the doorframes." [23] Joyce uses *crazy* in its etymological and now uncommon sense, once more indicating a physical condition.

Later, in a faded 1860 print showing two boxers, which Stephen sees, the "heavyweights in light loin cloths proposed gently each to other his bulbous fists." [24] Joyce again shifts a word which now is used almost invariably of mental transactions back to its physical origin and so infuses into it a new vigor. He does the same when, in a game of chess, "John Howard Parnell translated a white bishop gently." [25] *Translate* is in use today in this original sense of movement from one point to another, but it too is confined, usually to the immaterial change of emotions. Joyce drives it all the way back to its original meaning of picking up a concrete thing from a concrete rest, moving it across an intervening space, and bringing it down again on another concrete rest.

In addition to this trick of refreshing a word by pushing it back to an older, more palpable meaning, Joyce employs a grammatical device which is Elizabethan in the sense that it is an integral part of Elizabethan grammar and not of our own; namely, the changeability of parts of speech into one another, an adjective into a verb, a noun into an adverb, and so on, either in their existing forms or with syntactical modifications. [26] In the third

chapter, the *Proteus* episode, Stephen attempts to re-
capture the details of his dream: "After he woke me up
last night same dream or was it? Wait. Open hallway.
Street of harlots. Remember. Haroun al Raschid. I am
almosting it." [27] When Joyce read this scene to Budgen,
shortly after its composition, he remarked apropos of
almosting: "That's all in the Protean character of the thing.
Everything changes: land, water, dog, time of day. Parts
of speech change, too. Adverb becomes verb." [28] The
anastomosis of style and subject, which Stuart Gilbert [29]
has emphasized, makes this scene an occasion for an
unusual concentration of protean language, but this
Elizabethanism is a trick which Joyce also uses elsewhere.
In the episode of the newspaper office, a noun with a
slight change appears as an adverb: "—The ghost walks,
professor MacHugh murmured softly, biscuitfully to the
dusty windowpane." [30]

In this form of Elizabethanism Joyce does not revivify
old words; that is the function of the first form. Here he
generally creates new meanings for existing words by extending their usage to other parts of speech. Thus, his
renovation of language falls into two categories, the one
historical, the other creative.

For pure innovation, Joyce offers a mixed repertory.
The most prominent form, harking back to the early days
of his career when he first began to emphasize the sound
of words, is onomatopoeia. In the order, choice, and form
of words, Joyce always seeks to reproduce the experience
as closely as possible. Although this kind of experiment is
not entirely original, it has seldom if ever been carried
out on so extensive a scale.

As I have already suggested, onomatopoeia may be expressed in various ways, in the order of words, in their
choice, in their form. All three play an important part in
Ulysses and, in keeping with Joyce's theory of art, influence
the style of every chapter. The order of words is so important that without it whole sentences would be superfluous. Joyce, for example, not only writes a sentence in
imitation of a physical fact but repeats the information

in a second sentence, adding nothing new, yet, by a change
in order, heightening the imitation:

> Grossbooted draymen rolled barrels dullthudding out of
> Prince's stores and bumped them up on the brewery float.
> On the brewery float bumped dullthudding barrels rolled
> by grossbooted draymen out of Prince's stores.[31]

The dullthudding barrels roll bumping through the words.
And, again, Bloom, viewing a voluminous nape, conveys
to us the exact progress of his sight, putting us vicariously
through his experience: "Welts of flesh behind on him.
Fat folds of neck, fat, neck, fat, neck." [32]

In the choice of words, also, Joyce again and again
impresses the ear as well as the eye. Stephen on the strand
at Sandymount, watching the movement of a woman with
a bag, thinks: "She trudges, schlepps, trains, drags,
trascines her load." [33] Of this, Joyce remarked to Budgen:
"I like that crescendo of verbs . . . The irresistible tug
of the tides." [34] Tides or no tides, the vowels of the verbs
constitute a document in labor, growing steadily in
shrillness from the groaning guttural to an almost hysterical acuteness of effort. Even more striking, perhaps because it is not so elaborate, is the description of the clap
of thunder: "A black crack of noise in the street here,
alack, bawled back." [35] One sound, used with recurrence
and interval, evokes the crackling staccato of sudden,
loud, tearing thunder.

Then comes Joyce's experiment with the individual
word. In exerting every effort to render the experience in
as well as by means of the word, he inevitably meets some
which have not been recorded. The result is neologism.
The principle which underlies most of this production I
call dynamic onomatopocia. Joyce's remarkable gift for it
revcals itself throughout his work. For example, the cat in
Bloom's household, impatiently awaiting her morning
milk, utters a crescendo of protests:

> —Mkgnao! . . .
> —Mrkgnao! the cat cried. . . .
> —Mrkrgnao! the cat cried loudly.[36]

Later, at the burial of Paddy Dignam, Bloom indulges in one of his scientific vagaries:

> Have a gramophone in every grave or keep it in the house. After dinner on a Sunday. Put on poor old greatgrandfather Kraahraark! Hellohellohello amawfullyglad kraark awfully-gladaseeragain hellohello amarawf kopthsth.[37]

And in the brothel scene the waterfall at various points speaks, in harmony with the context:

> Poulaphouca Poulaphouca
> Poulaphouca Poulaphouca . . .
>
> Poulaphouca Poulaphouca
> Phoucaphouca Phoucaphouca . . .
>
> Phillaphulla Poulaphouca
> Poulaphouca Poulaphouca.[38]

The words which Joyce invents are all admirably suited to the speakers. The cat and the phonograph and the waterfall could hardly do better themselves.

However, Joyce not only invents new forms of onomatopoeia; he also strikes off the shackles which keep existing forms stiff and unmoving. In this connection, I met fully developed a notion of my own about the imperfect representation of onomatopoeic words. Some of them seemed to me extremely weak because they imitate an instant of experience instead of experience as process.

The danger of such novelty lies in exaggeration. As a "logical conclusion," a cant phrase in Joycean criticism, I should be justified in spelling *crash* with several pages of —*sh*'s to catch the sound of a vast ceiling which, loosening slowly, takes two or three minutes before all of it lies on the floor. But of excess I shall speak later. It is enough that in *Ulysses* one meets precisely this kind of word-building for the purpose of imitating process. Examples are numerous. Bloom, looking forward to his bath, sees "his trunk and limbs riprippled over." [39] In the Burton Restaurant, he witnesses: "A man spitting back on his plate: halfmasticated gristle: no teeth to chewchewchew it." [40] And, later, "Davy Byrne smiledyawnednodded all in one:

—Iiiiiichaaaaaaach!" [41]

Then there is the "endlessnessnessnessness" [42] of a chest-note in Simon Dedalus' rendition of *Martha*, and there is Molly Bloom's "wavyavyeavyheavyeavyevyevy hair un comb: 'd," [43] as there are later, in *Work in Progress*, "the hitherandthithering waters of" [44] the Liffey, and still later, in an article by Joyce, a "cry echechohoing." [45]

In all of these, the imitation is dynamic, extending over a period, reproducing duration, catching in the word the process. The reader who meets such experiments for the first time may find it difficult to acclimatize himself to their greater truthfulness. But with repetition the superior vitality of these words to that of their ancestors impresses itself upon the ear. One might recommend here the early practice of Stephen Dedalus:

> Words which he did not understand he said over and over to himself till he had learnt them by heart: and through them he had glimpses of the real world around him.[46]

Another form of innovation used by Joyce extensively is distortion. Words are rearranged, lengthened, shortened, often amputated to what D. H. Lawrence called "cabbage-stumps." [47] Thus, in the discussion on Shakespeare, the name of the librarian John Eglinton appears as littlejohn Eglinton, John sturdy Eglinton, Second Eglinton, *Eglintonus Chronolologos*, Mageeglinjohn, Judge Eglinton, Eglinton Johannes, and John Eclecticon. For cabbage-stumps the internal monologue is the most fertile soil. Here the characters, communing with themselves, utilize half-words and broken phrases with great frequency. Bloom is engrossed in a conundrum: "It is amusing to view the unpar one ar alleled embarra two ars is it? double ees [*sic*] ment of a harrassed pedlar while gauging au the symmetry of a peeled pear under a cemetery wall." [48]

The most important principle in the Ulyssean word-technique is the anastomosis of style and subject. Essentially this is onomatopoeia triumphant, commanding every possible means of reproducing the experience in words. To see this principle in action, *James Joyce's ULYSSES* is indispensable. Gilbert shows, in great detail, how the style and the vocabulary of every episode are determined by the matter. But, granting that the style and the subject are fused, no one can be expected to suffer through pages and pages on the argument that the style suits the subject and is therefore essential to the art. The votaries of Joyce acclaim whole sections of *Ulysses* because they adhere to this principle. If there is to be any judging of one thing by another, I prefer to judge theory by results.

The fusion of style with subject has given us some of the most successful of Joyce's chapters. The story of Bloom's encounter with the Citizen, couched in good mouth-filling Dublin idiom, is a superb piece of writing. And the master shines throughout the first half of the scene in which Gerty MacDowell's virginal bosom yields its secret yearnings—as Joyce says, "in a nambypamby jammy marmalady drawersy (alto la!) style with effects of incense mariolatry, masturbation, stewed cockles, painters' palette, chitchat, circumlocutions, etc., etc." [49]

On the other hand, Joyce in some of his *tours de force* falls flat. The section of parodies describing the scene at the hospital, for example, is a waste of effort. And the scene at Bloom's house after the delirium of nighttown, presented in the form of an examination paper! This sort of writing is full of the boredom which poisons the pleasure of the reader in other parts of *Ulysses*. Yet, one critic calls the examination paper one of the most fascinating chapters, observing that Joyce uses the Socratic method of question and answer!

With each chapter written in a language of its own, no better commentary is needed on the importance of the word in Joyce. As a result of this emphasis, Joyce's "sensibilities . . . have been developed far beyond those of his readers," [50] and he has ended by being unintelligible to all but himself—assuming that he has been spared the ordeal of Browning.

. . . and the Word was God.

In his zeal to present the whole of an experience *in* words, Joyce has, at last, presumed to give us not only the movement of chewchewchewing but also the halfmasticated gristle. Gilbert writes:

> . . . it is interesting to observe the Ulyssean word-technique carried a stage further in Mr Joyce's *Work in Progress*, where the mastication of food and its disintegration are reflected in a similar treatment of language, as in the following description of a copious meal. 'All the vitalmines is beginning to sozzle in chewn, fudgem, kates and epas and naboc and erics and oinnos on kingclud and xoxxoxo and xooxox xxoxoxxoxxx till I'm fustfed like fungstif.' Here the 'masticated' words can easily be reconstructed by the reader: *kates* being 'steak,' *kingclud* 'duckling,' *oinnos* 'onions' (with, perhaps, a tang of Greek wine) and so on. In the final stages of this metabolism alphabetic differences are reduced to a minimum, letters becoming mere noughts and crosses (vowels and consonants) and a mess of cabbage (xoxxoxo), followed by 'boiled protestants' *en purée* (with a dash of beef extract), completes the bellyful.[51]

Gilbert assures the reader that "here the 'masticated' words can easily be reconstructed," but it does not seem to have occurred to him that the reader may die in a good old age without knowing what Joyce is trying to do. Even if we suppose that the author's purpose is recognizable and that some of his gristle can be reintegrated, who is likely to recognize *xoxxoxo* as a mess of cabbage?

This is a logical conclusion of Joyce's word-technique. The *Portrait*, *Ulysses*, *Work in Progress*—each has been hailed at one time or another as the logical conclusion of Joyce's previous work. To such writing there is one final conclusion. Joyce will call his next work something like *Tabula Rasa* and regale the reader with hundreds of pages of closely bound paper, every one of which will be innocent of printer's ink, a commodity so ubiquitous and domineering that no modern literature has escaped it. Disciples will swarm to the defense of the Master, and learned commentaries will be spun out to show how superbly, how flawlessly, how incomparably James Joyce has rendered for all time the picture of the mind at that obscure moment in our embryological past before we are ushered into the world of sensation and idea—in short, the perfectly blank mind. Instead of Vico, the British Empiricists will be exhumed, in elaborate support of Joyce's position, of Joyce's form, choice, and order of space, of the degree of the whiteness of his page. The era of technique will then be not at an end but at its culmination, and all men will follow the Master, varying perhaps only in the number of pages, or, again, according to the intensity of their artistic vision, in the degree of the whiteness of the page. And it shall come to pass in that day that the great writer shall consort with the little, and the wolf shall dwell with the lamb, and the leopard shall lie down with the kid; and the calf and the young lion and the fatling together; and a little child shall read them.

BEFORE LEAVING IRELAND in 1904, Joyce announced that he would produce a great book within ten years. The boast was superbly fulfilled in A *Portrait of the Artist as a Young Man*. In 1944, three years after Joyce's death, Theodore Spencer edited, with an admirable introduction, a large portion of an early draft of this work, entitled *Stephen Hero* and written apparently between 1901 and 1906, during Joyce's last years at University College, Dublin, and first years on the Continent.

i

Stephen Hero is an absorbing document, straightforward, explicit, and marked by a fullness of statement which Joyce, for various reasons, denied to the *Portrait*. Covering about two of Stephen's university years, what we have of *Stephen Hero* has a better claim to the title *A Portrait of the Artist as a Young Man* than does the so-miscalled work, which treats Stephen's experience from his earliest memories to young manhood. The 383 pages of manuscript,[1] as the editor points out, coincide with the last 93 pages of the *Portrait*. In both versions Stephen is the same poor, arrogant, and solitary young man. The hero who, invited to contribute to a college review, asks, "And tell me, will I be paid?" is recognizable as the young man who, when invited to sign a testimonial for universal peace, asks, "—Will you pay me anything if I sign?" The hero who expects "reward from the public for [his] verses because [he] believe[s his] verses are to be numbered among the spiritual assets of the State" is recognizable as the young man who goes forth "to forge in the smithy of [his] soul the uncreated conscience of [his] race." And the hero who "professed scorn for the rabblement and contempt for authority," had a "commandment of reticence," "was very lonely," and lived "such a strange life—without help or sympathy from anyone" that "sometimes [he was] afraid of [himself]" is recognizable as the young man who felt keenly "that he was different from others," who "was happy only when he was . . . alone or in the company of phantasmal comrades," who "was destined to learn his own wisdom apart from others or to learn the wisdom of others himself wandering among the snares of the world."

It is notable that the youthful preferences which Joyce records in *Stephen Hero* are perhaps more significant than those he mentions in the *Portrait*. In *Stephen Hero*, as is not the case in the *Portrait*, we have a revealing account of Stephen's devotion to two artists. Of the first, Joyce begins: "It must be said simply and at once that at this time Stephen suffered the most enduring influence of his life." And Ibsen plays a central role in Stephen's experience, for it is in defense of him, in connection with a paper on "Art and Life" read before the University College Literary and Historical Society, that Stephen breaks a lance with the authority for which, as an artist, he professes contempt. Furthermore, in March, 1901, the nineteen-year-old Joyce wrote to Ibsen personally, praising "your highest excellence—your lofty impersonal power . . . and how in your absolute indifference to public canons of art, friends and shibboleths you walked in the light of your inward *heroism*." In October of the same year Joyce wrote, in the essay *The Day of the Rabblement*: "No man, said the Nolan, can be a lover of the true or the good unless he abhors the multitude; and the artist, though he may employ the crowd, is very careful to isolate himself"; he remarked that "every movement [of protest against the sterility and falsehood of the modern stage] that has set out *heroically* has achieved a little"; and he spoke reverently of "the old master who is dying in Christiania." I have italicized the words *heroism* and *heroically* for, written when *Stephen Hero* was presumably already in process of gestation, they indicate the turn of the author's thought at the time: Ibsen is a hero, and opposition to sterility and falsehood is the act of heroes to the prototype of Stephen the hero.

Of the second artist whose work Stephen admired, Joyce begins:

> [Stephen] had found on one of the carts of books near the river an unpublished book containing two stories by W. B. Yeats. One of these stories was called *The Tables of the Law* . . . and one evening while talking with a Capuchin, he had over and over to restrain an impulse which urged him to take the priest by the arm, lead him up and down the chapel-yard and deliver himself boldly of the whole story of *The Tables of the Law*, every word of which he remembered. . . . He satisfied himself by leading Lynch round the enclosure of Stephen's Green and making that young man very awkward by reciting Mr Yeats's story with careful animation. . . . He repeated often the story of *The Tables of the Law* and the story of the *Adoration of the Magi*.

Later, quotations from both stories are put into Stephen's mouth. And a further measure of Joyce's attachment to these stories is anonymously indicated in Yeats's prefatory note to the first public edition: "These two stories were privately printed some years ago. I do not think I should have reprinted them had I not met a young man in Ireland the other day, who liked them very much and nothing else that I have written." The young man, according to Yeats's biographer, Joseph Hone, was Joyce.

The leading characters of both stories stand outside established orders. Both artists whom Stephen and his creator find congenial are proud preachers of independence of social taboos. Joyce-Dedalus bears out a statement which Dedalus is later to make in *Ulysses:* "We walk through ourselves, meeting robbers, ghosts, giants, old men, young men, wives, widows, brothers-in-love. But always meeting ourselves."

Stephen's character, as I have said, is essentially the same in both versions. What changes is the relationship between that character and the author. This is perhaps the most important qualitative difference between the two versions.

A fair illustration of the attitude of the author to his subject in *Stephen Hero* is the introductory sentence, already quoted, about Ibsen (whom, it will be remembered, Joyce admired for his impersonality): "It must be said simply and at once that at this time Stephen suffered the most enduring influence of his life." Here is the author not merely reporting a fact regarding his character but also, by his strident emphasis, announcing his own position. Other brief editorial asides ("it is as well to admit that"—"undoubtedly") leave the reader no choice but to listen to the author's explicit point of view. The editorial phrase extends to sententious and abstract generalization:

> This quality of the mind which so reveals itself is called (when incorrigible) a decadence but if we are to take a general view of . . . the world we cannot but see a process to life through corruption. . . . When a demand for intelligent sympathy goes unanswered . . . he is a too stern disciplinarian who blames himself for having offered a dullard an opportunity to participate in the warmer movement of a more highly organized life. . . . No young man can contemplate the fact of death with extreme satisfaction and no young man, specialised by fate or her stepsister chance for an organ of sensitiveness and intellectiveness, can contemplate the network of falsities and trivialities which make up the funeral of a dead burgher without extreme disgust.

The tendency to editorialize reaches a peak, as one might expect, at a peak of emotion, and phrase and sentence are, in one instance, elaborated into a long and tense essay. Joyce has been reporting Stephen's thoughts on Catholicism.

That kind of Christianity which is called Catholicism seemed to him to stand in his way and forthwith he removed it. He had been brought up in the belief of the Roman supremacy and to cease to be a Catholic for him meant to cease to be a Christian.

Then, almost imperceptibly, Joyce crosses the vague line between autobiographical creation and creator:

The idea that the power of an empire is weakest at its borders requires some modification for everyone knows that the Pope cannot govern Italy as he governs Ireland nor is the Tsar as terrible an engine to the tradesmen of S. Petersburg as he is to the little Russian of the Steppes. In fact in many cases the government of an empire is strongest at its borders and it is invariably strongest there in the case when its power at the centre is on the wane. The waves of the rise and fall of empires do not travel with the rapidity of waves of light and it will be perhaps a considerable time before Ireland will be able to understand that the Papacy is no longer going through a period of anabolism. The bands of pilgrims who are shepherded safely across the continent by their Irish pastors must shame the jaded reactionaries of the eternal city by their stupefied intensity of worship in much the same way as the staring provincial newly arrived from Spain or Africa may have piqued the loyalty of some smiling Roman for whom . . . the future of his race was becoming uncertain as its past had already become obvious. Though it is evident on the one hand that this persistence of Catholic power in Ireland must intensify very greatly the loneliness of the Irish Catholic who voluntarily outlaws himself yet on the other hand the force which he must generate to propel himself out of so strong and intricate a tyranny may often be sufficient to place him beyond the region of re-attraction.

Again almost imperceptibly, Joyce crosses back from himself to his autobiographical creation:

It was, in fact, the very fervour of Stephen's former religious life which sharpened for him now the pains of his solitary position and at the same time hardened into a less pliable, a less appeasable enmity molten rages and glowing transports on which the emotions of helplessness and loneliness and despair had first acted as chilling influences.

It needed only a change of tense to transform the authorial essay into an organic part of Stephen's experience. But the young Joyce had not yet sufficiently detached himself from his own thoughts and feelings to give them to his not much younger creation. He failed, in other words, to achieve the "esthetic stasis" which Stephen regards as essential to the success of a work of art. "The artist, like the God of the creation," Stephen says in the *Portrait*, "remains within or behind or beyond or above his handiwork, invisible, refined out of existence, indifferent, paring his fingernails.—" In *Stephen Hero* a tone of adolescently turbulent rancor, everywhere audible, inspires the reader with loathing for "Irish paralysis"—a "kinetic" effect, which, according to Stephen's esthetic, makes for improper art. We may, in fact, say of the author of this early version what he says in it of his titular character: "It was hard for him to compel his head to preserve the strict temperature of classicism."

In the *Portrait*, on the other hand, from start to finish there is not a single comment or generalization; every thought, every feeling is particularly Stephen's. Now and then, to be sure, the author *reports* as author, but he never *comments*. "It was the very spirit of Ibsen himself," Joyce wrote in *Stephen Hero*, "that was discerned moving behind the impersonal manner of the artist"; so, again to be sure, it is the very spirit of Joyce himself that is discerned moving behind the impersonal manner of the artist of the *Portrait*. But such discernibleness is not inconsistent with the invisibility of the God of the creation behind his handiwork.

At this point the evolution of Joyce's novel becomes interesting beyond itself, for the history of this novel repeats the history of the genre. The change from *Stephen Hero* to the *Portrait* mirrors the progression from the novel of the overt and partisan manager to that of the invisible and impersonal director.

ii

The reader, however, will ask not only how far *Stephen Hero* generally resembles or differs from the

Portrait but also what it reveals about Joyce's work as a whole. I have already mentioned the explicitness of the earlier version; and the economy of the *Portrait* is a matter of common knowledge. As Spencer observed, *Stephen Hero* clarifies obscurities in Joyce's other works and illuminates Joyce's development as a craftsman.

To the examples of clarification cited by Spencer, I should like to add a few which point up Joyce's sometimes excessive economy.

Stephen Dedalus, having just refused to sign a petition for world peace—in the *Portrait*—mocks at a friend:

> —Now that you have signed the petition for universal peace—said Stephen—I suppose you will burn that little copybook I saw in your room.—
>
> As Davin did not answer Stephen began to quote:
> —Long pace, fianna! Right incline, fianna! Fianna, by numbers, salute, one, two!—
> —That's a different question—said Davin.—I'm an Irish nationalist, first and foremost. But that's you all out. You're a born sneerer, Stevie.—
> —When you make the next rebellion with hurley-sticks—said Stephen—and want the indispensable informer, tell me. I can find you a few in this college.—

Twenty-five pages earlier the reader has heard of Davin's attendance at a hurling match. Sixty pages later Stephen, having met Davin at a cigar-store, records in his diary: "He was in a black sweater and had a hurley-stick. . . . Just then my father came up. . . . Asked Davin if he might offer him some refreshment. Davin could not, was going to a meeting." Of hurley-sticks in the *Portrait* there is not another word. The reader may therefore be expected to see in Stephen's remark a bluntly contemptuous gibe inspired by the not clearly pertinent association of Davin with hurling. But let us look at a passage in *Stephen Hero* which is important enough to quote at some length:

> The meetings [of the nationalists] on Friday nights were public and were largely patronised by priests. The organisers brought in reports from different districts . . . when it was time for the whole company to break up all would rise and sing the Rallying-Song. . . . His [a certain

citizen's] circle was the separatist centre and in it reigned
the irreconcilable temper. It had its headquarters in
Cooney's tobacco-shop . . . To this circle Madden who
was the captain of a club of hurley-players reported the
muscular condition of the young irreconcilables under his
charge . . . A glowing example was to be found [in the
eyes of "these enthusiasts"] for Ireland in the case of
Hungary, an example, as these patriots imagined, of a long-
suffering minority, entitled by every right of race and
justice to a separate freedom, finally emancipating itself.
In emulation of that achievement bodies of young Gaels
conflicted murderously in the Phoenix Park with whacking
hurley-sticks, thrice armed in their just quarrel since
their revolution had been blessed for them by the
Anointed . . .

Stephen said one day to Madden:

—I suppose these hurley-matches and walking tours
are preparations for the great event.

—There is more going on in Ireland at present than
you are aware of.

—But what use are camàns [hurley-sticks]?

—Well, you see, we want to raise the physique of the
country.

With so clear and full a frame of reference—which must
have been in Joyce's mind as he wrote the *Portrait*—
Stephen's dull shaft would have been pointed and barbed.

And now for two brief specimens from *Ulysses*. In the
library scene, Stephen meditates: "Where is your brother?
Apothecaries' hall. My whetstone. Him, then Cranly,
Mulligan: now these." In the brothel scene Stephen calls
Lynch's cap "Whetstone!" The reader will comb *Ulysses*,
and the *Portrait* as well, for explanation in vain, for the
explanation is to be found in *Stephen Hero*, in which
"Stephen found Maurice [his brother] very useful for
raising objections."

In the second example from *Ulysses*, a passage which
makes good enough sense unbuttressed by further explanation is enriched by *Stephen Hero* with a new and clearly
pertinent association. In the brothel scene, Lynch's use of
the word *pandybat* precipitates the hallucination of Father

Dolan of Clongowes Wood College, which Stephen had attended as a child: "*Twice loudly a pandybat cracks, the coffin of the pianola flies open, the bald little round jack-in-the-box head of Father Dolan springs up.*" The immediate picture of the priest's head popping out of the pianola is enough, as I have indicated, to warrant the figure of the jack-in-the-box. But, again and again the hallucinations in the brothel scene, as we know, are based on reality. The vision of the priest's head is Stephen's, and *Ulysses* contains no clue to its origin. The full explanation of what must almost certainly have gone on in Joyce's mind as he wrote this passage is to be found in *Stephen Hero:*

> [Stephen's] mother told him one day that she had spoken of him to her confessor and asked his spiritual advice. Stephen turned to her and remonstrated hotly with her for doing such a thing.
>
> —It is a nice thing, he said, that you go and discuss me behind my back. Have you not your own nature to guide you, your own sense of what is right, without going to some Father Jack-in-the-Box to ask him to guide you?

To be sure, memories are carried over from the *Portrait* to *Ulysses* without explanation, and their full meaning for Stephen cannot possibly be arrived at without recourse to the earlier work. The practice may be justified on the ground that, since Stephen is in what, regarding his character, is a sequence of two novels, the reader may be expected to know the first novel before beginning the second—a justification tantamount to an admission that, as regards Stephen, *Ulysses* does not constitute an artistic whole, but some justification withal. What reason is there, however, in economy beyond comprehension on the basis of a work which the author, regarding it as juvenile, evidently did not intend to publish? Perhaps it may be urged that blind spots occupy a legitimate place in one's understanding of another mind. But since explanations for these particular spots did exist, surely blindness here is an unnecessary affliction.

As already indicated, *Stephen Hero* not only elucidates passages in Joyce's other works; it also prefigures Joyce's later activity—in particular, his development as a craftsman.

A brief description of Stephen's Uncle John may well contain the germ of the short story in *Dubliners* called "The Boarding House": "One of the boys' uncles was a very shock-headed asthmatic man who had in his youth been rather indiscreet with his landlady's daughter and the family had been scarcely appeased by a tardy marriage."

Stephen's remark "A man might think for seven years at intervals and all at once write a quatrain which would immortalise him seemingly without thought or care— seemingly" and a passing reference to "some ardent verses which he entitled a 'Vilanelle [sic] of the Temptress'" seem to represent the germ of the marvellously vivid record in the *Portrait* of the creation of a villanelle.

Again, the technique of a whole episode of *Ulysses* is adumbrated in the following passage:

> [Stephen] devised the following question and answer for the pseudo-classical catechism:
> Question—What great truth do we learn from the *Libation-Pourers* of Eschylus?
> Answer—We learn from the *Libation-Pourers* of Eschylus that in ancient Greece brothers and sisters took the same size in boots.

Here, in embryo, is the technique of the penultimate episode of *Ulysses*, the "impersonal" catechism which Joyce wrote with tongue in cheek.

Similarly, *Stephen Hero* anticipates the internal monologue of *Ulysses* more explicitly than does any part of the *Portrait*. We hear that "Cranly grew used to having sensations and impressions recorded and analysed before him [by Stephen] at the very instant of their apparition." The introspective habit, illustrated several times in the *Portrait*, is an appropriate base from which Joyce is later to find congenial the internal monologue in Dujardin's *Les*

Lauriers sont coupés and the probings of modern psychologists.

As early as *Stephen Hero*, also, Joyce's experiments with language are foreshadowed. Stephen "put his lines [of verse] together not word by word but letter by letter. He read Blake and Rimbaud on the values of letters and even permuted and combined the five vowels to construct cries for primitive emotions." A single passage from *Ulysses*, among countless passages, will suffice to make clear the importance of such experiment for Joyce's later work:

> Listen: a fourworded wavespecch: seesoo, hrss, rsseeiss ooos. Vehement breath of waters amid seasnakes, rearing horses, rocks. In cups of rocks it slops: flop, slop, slap: bounded in barrels. And, spent, its speech ceases.

The later master of the technique of juxtaposition for the effect of simultaneity [a brief specimen from a large number of passages employing the device is Bloom's thought "Excuse, miss, there's (whh!) just a (whh!) fluff"] is suggested in the powerful scene in which the urge to fornication with Emma Clery, and, immediately after it, the death of his sister press upon the artist the contradiction of beauty and mortality.

iii

Youthful and incomplete as it is, *Stephen Hero* should contribute substantially to Joyce's reputation. If, as I have said elsewhere, *Finnegans Wake* alienated some readers of Joyce, *Stephen Hero* may serve to remind them of two things. First, Joyce's earlier works—including the bulk of *Ulysses*, for people brought up on a literature produced largely under its influence—are eminently readable. Secondly, Joyce, who typifies the artist in exile, was paradoxically destined, as this youthful work intimates, to develop into one of the most significant spokesmen of his time.

Dealing with the turn of the century, the Irish Renaissance, the form of the novel, the establishment of modern drama, and such perennial questions as the psychology of the artist and of the work of art, and the relationship between the individual and the institutions of family, school, church, and state, *Stephen Hero* commands attention not only among admirers of Joyce but among all those interested in the history of the making of the modern mind.

3 HOMER'S ODYSSEY AND JOYCE'S ULYSSES

In *A Portrait of the Artist as a Young Man,* in large measure the log of Joyce's early literary navigations, Homer is not mentioned once. The strangeness of this fact can be appreciated only when one examines the influence of the *Odyssey* upon *Ulysses.* Stuart Gilbert has made this examination.[1] I am retracing the same ground for the purpose of further analysis. Gilbert, with the assistance of Joyce, points out a host of correspondences. I have discovered many others, and a considerable number of discrepancies.

First, then, let us recall the structure of the Homeric model. The *Odyssey* is divided into three parts, the *Telemachia,* the Adventures of Odysseus, and the *Nostos* (Return). The first part, through the fourth book, describes the plight of Telemachus in the lordless palace at Ithaca, in which the suitors of Penelope have taken up indefinite residence and wassailing. Telemachus is sent by Athene to Nestor and to Menelaus to inquire after his father, and Menelaus tells him his father's story, bringing it down to the sojourn of Odysseus with the nymph Calypso. Book V introduces Odysseus, whom Calypso, by divine command, is forced to send away on a raft of trees. Poseidon scatters the raft, Odysseus reaches the shore of the Phaeacians, who receive him hospitably, and, from Book VI through part of Book XIII, Odysseus is among the Phaeacians. At the request of King Alcinous, the guest tells his story, in Books IX–XIII. In the remaining books we have Odysseus' return to Ithaca, the massacre of the suitors, and the reunion with Penelope.

Following the same scheme, Joyce divides his work into three parts. The first, consisting of three episodes, describes the morning of Stephen Dedalus, the modern Telemachus. The central body of the work, beginning with the introduction of Odysseus in the person of Leopold Bloom in the fourth episode, corresponds to the wanderings of the Ithacan king, with what variations I shall show. And the last three episodes, in which Bloom, accompanied by Dedalus, returns to his home, correspond to the return of Odysseus. Joyce told Budgen:

> I am now writing a book . . . based on the wanderings of Ulysses. The Odyssey, that is to say, serves me as a ground plan. Only my time is recent time and all my hero's wanderings take no more than eighteen hours.[2]

Later he spoke of his book as a "modern Odyssey" (*ibid.*, p. 20).

This, however, does not tell the whole story. The title of each episode, nowhere indicated in the text of *Ulysses*, is either a Homeric personage or incident. Thus we have, in order: *Telemachus, Nestor, Proteus, Calypso, The Lotus-eaters, Hades, Aeolus, The Lestrygonians, Scylla and Charybdis, The Wandering Rocks, The Sirens, The Cyclops, Nausicaa, The Oxen of the Sun, Circe, Eumaeus, Ithaca,* and *Penelope*. In addition, each episode is individualized and its Homeric correspondence reinforced by scene, hour, organ of the human body, art, symbol, technique, and, occasionally, color.[3] The apparent chaos of *Ulysses* is in reality a carefully integrated system.

A cursory examination of the Homeric correspondences will show that they are neither chronological nor proportionate. First, as to chronology. The most glaring inconsistencies, from the standpoint of Homeric order, occur in the central portion of the book. Of twelve episodes only two, the seventh and the eighth, are in the same order as their Homeric parallels. Episode by episode, the correspondence takes the following course through the

Odyssey: Books IV and V, IX, XI, X, X, XII, XII, XII (the last three in reverse order and with the addition of an experience which Odysseus avoids), IX, VI, XII, and X. This meandering route bears witness to the fact that Joyce did not commit himself to an exact reproduction of the course of Homer's narrative. It seems rather as if, in his quest for incident on which to hang the thoughts of his characters, Joyce took the adventures of Odysseus and his associates only as a starting-point and arranged them to suit his own purposes. Thus, as I have indicated, he reversed the order in which the episodes *Scylla and Charybdis, The Wandering Rocks,* and *The Sirens* stand in the *Odyssey,* and in the second of the three added an experience which Odysseus avoided entirely. The episodes *The Lotus-eaters* and *The Cyclops,* which fall consecutively in the ninth book of the *Odyssey,* are separated by six others in *Ulysses.* And as a crowning example of Joyce's departure from his model, the Oxen of the Sun, about which Circe warns Odysseus in advance, in *Ulysses* form the theme of the episode immediately preceding the parallel with the story of Circe. So much for chronology.

Secondly, as to proportion. Here Joyce's departures are even more striking. Again, the best examples are to be found in the central section of the book. The subject of the Lestrygonians, to which Homer devotes a paragraph about a page and half long,[4] Joyce builds into an episode of thirty-three pages. The Wandering Rocks, which occupy a half paragraph in Homer, are expanded to an episode of thirty-six pages. The three episodes *Scylla and Charybdis, The Wandering Rocks,* and *The Sirens* in Joyce occupy 105 out of a total of 768 pages, in Homer 8 out of a total of 383.

In addition to differences of chronology and proportion, there is one notable instance in which Joyce proves himself as a craftsman distinctly inferior to his ancient predecessor. I refer to the transition from the first to the second parts of their works. Joyce, following the first four books of Homer, presents Stephen Dedalus, Telemachus, in his first three episodes, and in the next introduces Bloom, his

Odysseus. The time of the first three episodes and of the second three is identical: eight, ten, and eleven o'clock in the morning, respectively. Until the fourth episode we see nothing and hear nothing of Bloom; but at eleven o'clock, without any warning, we are abruptly dragged back to eight, to begin the day all over again with him. In Homer, however, the *Telemachia* and the Adventures of Odysseus are organically related by Menelaus' recital, in the fourth book, of the story of Odysseus up to his sojourn with Calypso. This leads logically to the appearance of Odysseus, in the next book, on the isle of Ogygia and to the inauguration of his wanderings.

I pass to more detailed observations on the individual episodes. In the first episode, besides the recurrent allusions to Greek words, names, and notions—"Chrysostomos" and Dedalus' "absurd name, an ancient Greek," [5] the "Hellenic ring" of the name of Malachi Mulligan and his desire to "go to Athens" (*ibid.*, p. 6), his cry of *"Thalatta! Thallatta!"* [sic] [6] and his wish to "Helenise" [sic] the island (*ibid.*, p. 9)—there are a number of immediate recalls of the language of the first book of the *Odyssey*. Mulligan's *"Epi oinopa ponton"* (*ibid.*, p. 7; repeated, p. 565) and the use of the term *omphalos* (*ibid.*, pp. 9, 19) echo the "wine-dark sea" (*Odyssey*, p. 6) and "the navel of the sea" (*ibid.*, p. 2). To the significance of the *omphalos* in *Ulysses* Gilbert devotes a number of pages (48–53), failing, however, to note that the term is actually used in the corresponding book of the *Odyssey*. It seems reasonable to assume that Joyce, working in parallels, would have the corresponding book uppermost in mind. The reader who knows his *Odyssey*, then, will remember that Telemachus spoke to Athene of those "that devour the livelihood of another without atonement" (p. 6), when he hears Buck Milligan chant:

> —*If anyone thinks that I amn't divine*
> *He'll get no free drinks when I'm making the wine*
> *But have to drink water and wish it were plain*
> *That I make when the wine becomes water again.*
>
> [*Ulysses*, p. 20.]

or that Athene flew away "like an eagle of the sea" (*Odyssey*, p. 10; cf. also p. 40) when he reads the following of Mulligan:

> He tugged swiftly at Stephen's ashplant in farewell and, running forward to a brow of the cliff, fluttered his hands at his sides like fins or wings of one about to rise in the air. . . .
> He capered before them down towards the fortyfoot hole, fluttering his winglike hands, leaping nimbly, Mercury's hat quivering in the fresh wind that bore back to them his brief birdlike cries. [*Ulysses*, pp. 20–21.]

In the second episode, *Nestor*, corresponding to the second and third books of the *Odyssey*, Joyce translates the ancient story into modern terms at least three times. It will be recalled that Mentor chides the suitors for their violence to the household of Odysseus and is berated in turn (*Odyssey*, p. 22). The old man, impatient and angry, is reproduced in Mr. Deasy, who seems to combine in himself the qualities of both Mentor and Nestor:

> When he had reached the schoolhouse voices again contending called to him. He turned his angry white moustache.
> —What is it now? he cried continually without listening. . . .
> And as he stepped fussily back across the field his old man's voice cried sternly:
> —What is the matter? What is it now?
> Their sharp voices cried about him on all sides: their many forms closed round him, the garish sunshine bleaching the honey of his illdyed head. [*Ulysses*, p. 30.]

After the assembly, Telemachus steps down "into the vaulted treasure-chamber of his father, a spacious room, where gold and bronze lay piled, and raiment in coffers, and fragrant olive oil in plenty" (*Odyssey*, p. 25). This chamber is described in parallel fashion by Joyce when Mr. Deasy pays Stephen his monthly salary:

> —First, our little financial settlement, he said.
> He brought out of his coat a pocketbook bound by a leather thong. It slapped open and he took from it two

notes, one of joined halves, and laid them carefully on the
table.

—Two, he said, strapping and stowing his pocketbook
away.

And now his strongroom for the gold. Stephen's em-
barrassed hand moved over the shells heaped in the cold
stone mortar: whelks and money cowries and leopard
shells: and this, whorled as an emir's turban, and this, the
scallop of Saint James. An old pilgrim's hoard [Odysseus
is recalled here, of course], dead treasure, hollow shells.
[*Ulysses*, p. 30.]

Both Telemachus and Stephen replenish their supply of
treasure.[7]

In the discussion which follows, between Mr. Deasy
and Stephen, the schoolmaster has this to say about the
Jews: "They sinned against the light . . . And you can
see the darkness in their eyes. And that is why they are
wanderers on the earth to this day" (*Ulysses*, pp. 34–35).
Later, Mr. Deasy mentions by name the "war on Troy"
(p. 35). Odysseus' men, too, sinned against the light, and
they, too, wandered: "For through the blindness of their
own hearts they perished, fools, who devoured the oxen
of Helios Hyperion: but the god took from them their
day of returning" (*Odyssey*, p. 1).

The last episode of the prelude, called *Proteus* and
corresponding to the fourth book of the *Odyssey*, contains
two Homeric recalls.[8] First, Nestor, hearing the voice of
Telemachus, says: "amazement comes upon me as I look
at thee; for verily thy speech is like unto his [Odysseus'];
none would say that a younger man would speak so like
an elder" (*ibid.*, p. 33). Later Helen and Menelaus
marvel at the likeness of son to father (*ibid.*, p. 49).
Stephen, on the strand, reflects: "Wombed in sin darkness
I was too, made not begotten. By them, the man with
my voice and my eyes and a ghostwoman with ashes on
her breath" (*Ulysses*, p. 39). And, like Nestor and
Menelaus a contemporary of the father, Kevin Egan in
Paris said to Stephen: "You're your father's son. I know
the voice" (*ibid.*, p. 44; cf. p. 643). Secondly, Telemachus

does not wish to sleep in the palace of Nestor (*Odyssey*, p. 39); and Stephen thinks: "I will not sleep there [at the Martello tower] when this night comes" (*Ulysses*, p. 45).

With the entrance of Leopold Bloom in the next episode, Odysseus himself comes upon the scene, and Joyce finds new opportunities for Homeric recalls, at least one of which has not been pointed out. Both Odysseus and Bloom make use, practical and theoretical respectively, of olive trees (*Odyssey*, p. 85; *Ulysses*, p. 60).

The Lotus-eaters, Joyce's fifth episode, contains one distinct recall of Homer, this time in anticipation of the next episode, which parallels Odysseus' descent into Hades. Odysseus meets Elpenor, whose body is still unburied, and Elpenor asks Odysseus to bury it (*Odyssey*, pp. 163–64). M'Coy, who will not attend the funeral of Paddy Dignam, and who seems to share with Dignam correspondence to Elpenor, asks Bloom to do him a favor (*Ulysses*, p. 74). Odysseus answers: "All this, luckless man, will I perform for thee and do" (*Odyssey*, *loc. cit.*). Bloom answers: "That will be done" (*Ulysses*, *loc. cit.*).

The atmosphere of death and of Hades is built up both by Homer and by Joyce. In the *Odyssey*, the eleventh book is largely a list of the spirits seen by Odysseus; in *Ulysses*, also, we have a list:

> Mr Bloom's glance travelled down the edge of the paper, scanning the deaths. Callan, Coleman, Dignam, Fawcett, Lowry, Naumann, Peake, what Peake is that? is it the chap was in Crosbie and Alleyne's? no, Sexton, Urbright. [*Ibid.*, p. 90.]

Odysseus, describing the sight of the spirits, says:

> . . . lo, the spirits of the dead that be departed gathered them from out of Erebus. Brides and youths unwed and old men of many and evil days, and tender maidens with grief yet fresh at heart; and many there were, wounded with bronze-shod spears, men slain in fight with their bloody mail about them. And these many ghosts flocked together from every side about the trench with a wondrous cry, and pale fear gat hold on me. [*Odyssey*, p. 163.]

The funeral carriage bearing Bloom and his fellows steered left for Finglas road.

> The stone cutter's yard on the right. Last lap. Crowded on the spit of land silent shapes appeared, white, sorrowful, holding out calm hands, knelt in grief, pointing. Fragments of shapes, hewn. In white silence: appealing. [*Ulysses*, p. 98.]

A little further:

> The high railings of Prospects rippled past their gaze. Dark poplars, rare white forms. Forms more frequent, white shapes thronged amid the trees, white forms and fragments streaming by mutely, sustaining vain gestures on the air. [*Ibid.*, p. 99.]

And Bloom, praying for the dead, reflects:

> Every mortal day a fresh batch: middleaged men, old women, children, women dead in childbirth, men with beards, baldheaded business men, consumptive girls with little sparrow's breasts. [*Ibid.*, p. 103.]

Homer's list is especially akin to the last.

Against this background, so like Homer's, Joyce recounts the death of his Elpenor. Bloom, as usual, is monologizing, about Paddy Dignam:

> Blazing face: redhot. Too much John Barleycorn. Cure for a red nose. Drink like the devil till it turns adelite. A lot of money he spent colouring it.
>
> Mr Power gazed at the passing houses with rueful apprehension.
>
> —He had a sudden death, poor fellow, he said.
>
> —The best death, Mr Bloom said.
>
> Their wide open eyes looked at him.
>
> —No suffering, he said. A moment and all is over. Like dying in sleep. [*Ibid.*, p. 94.]

With this compare Elpenor's account of his death:

> Son of Laertes, of the seed of Zeus, Odysseus of many devices, an evil doom of some god was my bane and *wine out of measure*. When I laid me down on the housetop of Circe I minded me not to descend again by the

way of the tall ladder, but fell right down from the roof, and my neck was broken off from the bones of the spine, and my spirit went down to the house of Hades. [*Odyssey*, pp. 163–64; italics supplied.]

The incident of Aeolus, to which Joyce devotes a whole episode, in the *Odyssey* occupies less than three pages. Among many echoes, I have found more than a half dozen not previously noted. In four cases they are clear. Two of the headlines strewn through the episode read "O, HARP EOLIAN" (*Ulysses*, p. 126) and "SOPHIST WALLOPS HAUGHTY HELEN SQUARE ON PROBOSCIS. SPARTANS GNASH MOLARS. ITHACANS VOW PEN IS CHAMP" (*ibid.*, p. 147). Stephen recalls a fragment of Mr. Deasy's remarks: "For Helen, the runaway wife of Menelaus, ten years the Greeks" (*ibid.*, p. 131). And Professor MacHugh discourses on the Greeks (*ibid.*, p. 132). Besides these obvious recalls, Joyce makes use of several implied correspondences. Aeolus' children "feast evermore by their dear father and their kind mother, and dainties innumerable lie ready to their hands" (*Odyssey*, p. 144). One of the early headlines reads "AND IT WAS THE FEAST OF THE PASSOVER" (*Ulysses*, p. 121). The winds of Aeolus are personified by the scampering, boisterous newsboys, subjects of the editor Crawford, the modern Aeolus: "Screams of newsboys barefoot in the hall rushed near and the door was flung open" (*ibid.*, p. 127). "The troop of bare feet was heard rushing along the hallway and pattering up the staircase" (*ibid.*, p. 141). "The first newsboy came pattering down the stairs at their heels and rushed out into the street, yelling" (*ibid.*, p. 142). "Another newsboy shot past them, yelling as he ran" (*ibid.*, p. 143). "A bevy of scampering newsboys rushed down the steps, scampering in all directions, yelling, their white papers fluttering" (*ibid.*, p. 144). "Mr Bloom, breathless, caught in a whirl of wild newsboys . . ." (*ibid.*). And later in the day Bloom, not far from Gerty MacDowell, recalls the newsboys who made him "awkward" (*ibid.*, p. 369). When the newsboys rush near in their first appearance and the door is flung open, the editor says: "There's a hurricane blowing" (*ibid.*,

p. 127). This parallels exactly the text of the *Odyssey*, where "They loosed the wallet, and all the winds [here the newsboys] brake forth" is followed immediately by "And the violent blast seized my men" (p. 145). Again Joyce follows Homer closely under the consecutive head-lines "EXIT BLOOM" and "A STREET CORTEGE" (*Ulysses*, p. 128). Odysseus says: "But when I in turn took the word and asked of my journey, and bade him send me on my way, he too denied me not, but furnished an escort" (*Odyssey*, p. 144). Bloom takes the word: "—I'm just running round to Bachelor's walk, Mr Bloom said, about this ad of Keyes's. Want to fix it up. They tell me he's round there in Dillon's." Bloom's hesitation ("He looked indecisively for a moment at their faces") asks of his journey and bids them—chiefly, of course, the editor, whom he addresses—send him on his way. The editor's cry of "Begone! . . . The world is before you" denies him not. And "the file of capering newsboys in Mr Bloom's wake, the last zigzagging white on the breeze a mocking kite, a tail of white bowknots," forms the escort. Further-more, like Aeolus, Crawford grows angry at Bloom's re-turn. We first hear of this when Bloom returns over the telephone: "—Tell him to go to hell, the editor said promptly" (*Ulysses*, p. 135). And Crawford improves on his anger when Bloom returns in person (*ibid.*, p. 145). Odysseus returns to beg a wind of Aeolus, beseeching him in soft words (*Odyssey*, p. 146). Bloom returns to ask Crawford, in conciliatory tones, for "just a little puff" (*Ulysses*, p. 144). Both suffer explosive replies. At once, now near the end of the incident, Bloom, the modern Odysseus, thinks: "Look out for squalls" (*ibid.*, p. 145), and two headlines further we read "RAISING THE WIND" (*ibid.*).

"*Lestrygonians*," Joyce said to Budgen, ". . . corre-sponds to the adventure of Ulysses with the cannibals. My hero is going to lunch. But there is a seduction motive in the Odyssey, the cannibal king's daughter. Seduction appears in my book as women's silk petticoats hanging in a shop window" (Budgen, p. 20). However, Gilbert, who, as I have indicated, wrote his commentary with the assistance of Joyce, says: "The callous king Antiphates is symbolized by Mr Bloom's imperious hunger; the sight and reek of food are the decoy, his daughter . . ." (p. 190). The inconsistency is perhaps explainable as a bifurcation of correspondence. Joyce may have intended both the petticoats and the sight and reek of food to symbolize the seduction motive, and it is quite possible that in assisting Gilbert, years after the conversation with Budgen, he had forgotten his earlier intention. As for other correspondences in this episode, I think we may accept 1 P.M., its time, as the time of the "midday meal" (*Odyssey*, p. 148) which Antiphates made ready with one of Odysseus' company; the near destruction of Bloom and his companions under horses' hoofs (*Ulysses*, p. 160) as a counterpart of the near destruction of Odysseus and all his companions (*Odyssey*, *loc. cit.*), and the mention of cannibals (*Ulysses*, p. 169) as an obviously relevant allusion.

The general Homeric correspondences of the next episode, *Scylla and Charybdis*, are symbolic and recondite to the point of futility. Gilbert says:

> The *motifs* of the sheer, steadfast rock of Scylla and the restless whirlpool of Charybdis, a sea of troubles, are utilized in a symbolic sense in this episode. The stability of Dogma, of Aristotle and of Shakespeare's Stratford are contrasted with the whirlpool of Mysticism, Platonism, the London of Elizabethan times. Shakespeare, Jesus and Socrates, like Ulysses, the man of balanced genius, pass bravely out, though not unscathed, from between these perils of the soul. 'A man passed out between them, bowing, greeting.' The departure of Mr Bloom from the metaphysical twilight of the library into a 'shattering daylight of no thoughts' symbolizes such an escape. [p. 204.]

How tenuous this symbolism is may be gauged from the fact that Bloom does not take part at all in the discussion about Shakespeare, so that there is no Scylla and Charybdis between which he, like Odysseus, may pass. Perhaps it is in compensation for this tenuousness that this episode contains one of the rare allusions to Homer himself (*Ulysses*, p. 185) and another allusion to a grey-eyed goddess (p. 189), clearly a recall of Athene, who is so described repeatedly by Homer (*e.g., Odyssey*, p. 2).

With regard to the next episode, *The Wandering Rocks*, I must take exception to two statements by Gilbert. First, he says: "In this episode, Mr Bloom excels his great precursor, for he accepts a supplementary adventure which the latter declined" (p. 214). It argues no excellence in a man if he invites certain destruction for no good reason (see *Odyssey*, p. 183). And it is only by making Circe out to be wrong and distorting the inevitable parallel that Joyce can have Bloom pass through safely. The second exception concerns a matter of fact. Gilbert speaks of "the Homeric conception of these rocks, clashing together at regular intervals" (p. 215), whereas the only clashing mentioned in Homer takes place between "the beetling rocks" on the one side and "the great wave" (*Odyssey, loc. cit.*) on the other. However, the episode itself, divided into nineteen contemporaneous fragments about various people in various parts of Dublin and joined by the interpolation of retrospective or anticipatory excerpts from one fragment into another, achieves the effect of wandering.

In *The Sirens* we return to more literal correspondence with Homer. Bloom again deviates from the example of his predecessor, this time by omission. Whereas Odysseus makes every effort to return to Ithaca, taking precautions against undue detention by the Sirens (in spite of the fact that he listens to their flattering invitations), Bloom does not ignore the Sirens, whom Joyce reduces first to two barmaids and finally, by implication, to two whores. Circe warns Odysseus: "Whoso draws nigh them unwittingly and hears the sound of the Sirens' voice, never doth he see wife or babes stand by him on his return, nor have they joy at his coming" (*ibid.*, p. 183). This describes Bloom's situation. While he is listening to Miss Kennedy and Miss Douce, he is replaced in Molly's favors by Blazes Boylan, and Molly would have no joy, in more than one sense, at Poldy's coming. So Bloom thinks:

Thou lost one. All songs on that theme. Yet more Bloom stretched his string. Cruel it seems. Let people get fond of each other: lure them on. Then tear asunder. . . . Forgotten. I too. [*Ulysses*, p. 273.]

And later:

I too, last my race. Milly young student. Well, my fault perhaps. No son. Rudy. Too late now. Or if not? If not? If still?

He bore no hate.

Hate. Love. Those are names. Rudy. Soon I am old. [*Ibid.*, p. 280.]

To remind us further of the Sirens, Miss Douce attracts and holds the attention of a passerby who is, significantly, "killed looking back" (*ibid.*, p. 253); Miss Douce reproduces the Sirens' "field of flowers" (*Odyssey*, p. 185) in the flower which she wears (*Ulysses*, p. 254); a poster represents a mermaid (*ibid.*, p. 259); one of the barmaids holds Bloom (*ibid.*, pp. 259–60), like Odysseus (*Odyssey*, pp. 186–87), in talk; both barmaids preen themselves (*Ulysses*, p. 260); Miss Douce 'seizes her prey easily' (*ibid.*, p. 261) and sings an oceansong (*ibid.*), and the character of the Sirens is finally reduced to that of a streetwalker (*ibid.*, pp. 285–86).

The incident of the Cyclops, one of the longer episodes of the *Odyssey* (pp. 129–43), becomes in *Ulysses* an opportunity for some of Joyce's most successful humor, owing a large part of its success, like the first half of the next episode, to its complete intelligibility. Odysseus describes Polyphemus as

a man . . . of monstrous size, who shepherded his flocks alone and afar, and was not conversant with others, but dwelt apart in lawlessness of mind. Yea, for he was a monstrous thing and fashioned marvellously, nor was he like to any man that lives by bread, but like a wooded peak of the towering hills, which stands out apart and alone from others [p. 131],

a man in whose presence the Achaeans' "heart . . . was broken for terror of the deep voice and his own monstrous shape" (p. 133). In one of the early inflated sections of this episode, Joyce's long description of his Cyclops seems to have drawn on Homer's for its mountain imagery:

> From shoulder to shoulder he measured several ells and his rocklike mountainous knees were covered, as was likewise the rest of his body wherever visible, with a strong growth of tawny prickly hair in hue and toughness similar to the mountain gorse (*Ulex Europeus*). [*Ulysses*, p. 291.]

The chimney sweep who almost gouged out the eye of the narrator with his brush (*ibid.*, p. 287) seems to wield a miniature of Polyphemus' club, which, "of olive wood, yet green" (*Odyssey*, p. 135), still has something of the brush about it. The club is next inflated to "a mighty cudgel rudely fashioned out of paleolithic stone" (*Ulysses*, p. 292). The Cyclops' herds (*Odyssey*, pp. 132–33) are echoed in the following passage in Joyce:

> And by that way wend the herds innumerable of bellwethers and flushed ewes and shearling rams and lambs and stubble geese and medium steers and roaring mares and polled calves and longwools and storesheep . . . [pp. 289–90].

The Citizen's "We want no more strangers in our house" (p. 318) is easily recognizable as a recall of Polyphemus' xenophobia. Both have a love for wine (*Odyssey*, p. 136; *Ulysses*, p. 290); both are served three times (*Odyssey*, p. 137; *Ulysses*, pp. 290, 309, 325). In contrast with their drinking is the abstinence of Bloom, "the prudent member" (*Ulysses*, p. 292; see also p. 298), whose prudence is emphasized in this episode in a way that is comparable to the emphasis on Odysseus' cunning in his relation to Polyphemus.[9] And both Odysseus and Bloom sacrifice prudence to temper in taunting their former tormentors, in spite of dissuading companions (*Odyssey*, p. 141; *Ulysses*, p. 336). After the blinding of Polyphemus, "the ewes bleated unmilked about the pens, for their udders were swollen to bursting" (*Odyssey*, p. 139). In the description of the herds in *Ulysses* already quoted, the "udders" of these cattle also "are distended with superabundance of milk and butts of butter and rennets of cheese and farmer's firkins" (*Ulysses*, p. 290), and so on. The anonymity of Odysseus is divided—another example of bifurcation—between the narrator and, by a reversal of the Odyssean relationship, the Citizen. Odysseus under the ram is recalled when the Citizen calls Bloom "a wolf in sheep's clothing" (*ibid.*, p. 332) and when the narrator calls Bloom "old sheepsface" (*ibid.*, p. 339). In keeping with Joyce's awareness of comic effects is the reduction of the Olympian Poseidon (*Odyssey*, p. 142) to the condition of a sicked dog (*Ulysses*, p. 339).

Moreover, comic effect in this episode commands a device all its own, the technique of gigantism. The narrator's Dublin idiom is interrupted periodically and the story recast against a grand background in a highly inflated style. The roots of this technique lie in the *Odyssey* itself, and in some instances, one of which I have already noted, the same roots are cultivated by Joyce. Polyphemus is "like a wooded peak of the towering hills, which stands out apart and alone from others" (*Odyssey*, p. 131). The doorstone to his cave is "such an one as two and twenty good four-wheeled wains could not raise from the ground" (*ibid.*, p. 133). The club is "likened . . . in size to the mast of a black ship of twenty oars, a wide merchant vessel that traverses the great sea gulf" (*ibid.*, p. 135). And when it is thrust into Polyphemus' eye, Odysseus says:

> I from my place aloft turned it about, as when a man bores a ship's beam with a drill while his fellows below spin it with a strap, which they hold at either end, and the auger runs round continually . . . the roots [of Polyphemus' eyeball] . . . crackled in the flame. And as when a smith dips an axe or adze in chill water with a great hissing . . . even so did his eye hiss round the stake of olive [pp. 137–38].

Homer employs the same device in reverse when Odysseus says: "he . . . laid his hands upon my fellows, and clutching two together dashed them, as they had been whelps, to the earth . . ." (p. 134), and again when, after driving his flocks forth from the cave, Polyphemus set the great doorstone in its place "as one might set the lid on a quiver" (p. 135). The comic function of Joyce's gigantism is clearly apparent from the concluding sentence of the episode: "And they beheld Him even Him, ben Bloom Elijah, amid clouds of angels ascend to the glory of the brightness at an angle of forty-five degrees over Donohoe's in Little Green Street like a shot off a shovel" (*Ulysses*, p. 339).

In passing from his analysis of *The Cyclops* to *Nausicaa* Gilbert says: "Here [in *Nausicaa*], after the volcanic rages of the Cyclops' den and a miraculous escape from seismic catastrophe, rest comes at last to the stormtossed heart of Mr Bloom" (p. 259). A glance at the *Odyssey* reveals another discrepancy between Joyce's work and its model, for rest does not come to Odysseus among the Phaeacians after the episode of the Cyclops, but after storm and shipwreck. The encounter with Polyphemus takes place three books after that with Nausicaa in Homer's narrative and more than seven years—the length of Odysseus' stay with Calypso—earlier in the experience of Odysseus. The entire sojourn of Odysseus with the Phaeacians runs from Book VI through part of Book XIII of the *Odyssey*. His direct association with Nausicaa is explicitly stated only in Book VI and in a short passage of Book VIII (p. 122). However, the length of his stay cannot be measured in terms of so many books, first, because time and space are not proportionate in the *Odyssey*, secondly, because Books IX–XII represent narration by Odysseus in the tradition of the hero guest. Odysseus' recital provides ten episodes for Joyce's wanderer, which Joyce prefers to have him live rather than report. Quantitatively, this represents Joyce's greatest departure from Homer; technically, perhaps his wisest.

In the episode of *Nausicaa*, according to both works, the heroine is attended by girl companions (*ibid.*, p. 89; *Ulysses*, p. 340). Nausicaa's brothers, the three "lusty bachelors" (*Odyssey*, p. 88), are reproduced in "the baby in the pushcar, and Tommy and Jacky Caffrey, two little curlyheaded boys, dressed [probably like their nautical prototypes] in sailor suits with caps to match and the name H. M. S. Belleisle printed on both" (*Ulysses, loc. cit.*); they prove their lustiness in short order. Nausicaa herself is, in the one version, "a maiden like to the gods in form and comeliness" (p. 86), in the other "as fair a specimen of winsome Irish girlhood as one could wish to see" (p. 342). In the one version she is told in a dream: "Lo, already they are wooing thee, the noblest youths of all the Phaeacians, among that people whence thou thyself dost draw thy lineage" (p. 87); in the other she dreams waking:

> Had kind fate but willed her to be born a gentlewoman of high degree in her own right and had she only received the benefit of a good education Gerty MacDowell might easily have held her own beside any lady in the land and have seen . . . patrician suitors at her feet vying with one another to pay their devoirs to her [p. 342].

"Even so the girl Nausicaa unwed outshone her maiden company" (p. 89); "of a surety God's fair land of Ireland did not hold her equal" (p. 343). Ciss, like any Phaeacian handmaid, would give "anything for a quiet life" (p. 347; cf. *Odyssey*, p. 92: "That mortal . . . to the gods"). Nausicaa is "ashamed to speak of glad marriage to her father" (p. 88); Gerty "bent down her head and crimsoned at the idea of Cissy saying an unladylike thing like that out loud she'd be ashamed of her life to say" (p. 347). Odysseus prays to the virgin Nausicaa as to divine Artemis "after many trials and sore" (p. 91); the men participating in the temperance retreat meet "in that simple fane beside the waves, after the storms of this weary world, kneeling before the feet of the immaculate . . . the old familiar words, holy Mary holy virgin of virgins" (pp. 347–48; cf. p. 348: "And still the voices . . . most merciful"). Both Nausicaa and Gerty fumble the ball in the celebrated game (*Odyssey*, pp. 89–90; *Ulysses*, p. 349). Both display their clean undergarments (*Odyssey*, p. 89; *Ulysses*, pp. 359–60, and cf. p. 362: "Lingerie does it"). Both bid farewell with identical meaning to the parting guest. Nausicaa says: "Farewell, stranger, and even in thine own country bethink thee of me upon a time, for that to me first thou owest the ransom of life" (p. 122). Gerty's gesture is interpreted by Bloom in the same vein: "Why she waved her hand. I leave you this to think of me when I'm far away on the pillow" (p. 368). Finally, Odysseus' lot is translated into the internal monologue of Bloom as follows:

> Dreadful life sailors have . . . Married too. Sometimes away for years at the ends of the earth somewhere . . . Wife in every port they say. She has a good job if she minds it till Johnny comes marching home again. If ever he does. . . . How can they like the sea? Yet they do [pp. 371–72].

From the seashore Bloom makes his way, in a maze of "piplodocan [sic] periods which correspond to the reptilian stage of human and embryonic evolution" (Gilbert, p. 278), to the lying-in hospital.

The most prominent departure from the Homeric pattern in this episode is the meeting of Bloom and Stephen; in the *Odyssey*, father and son are reunited only in the hut of Eumaeus. The implications of this change for the next episode in Joyce are even more novel, for Telemachus there joins his father in the pleasures of the isle of Aia. Yet, like its predecessors, the episode is studded with recalls of the corresponding section of the *Odyssey*. Eurylochus, pleading for a call on the port of Thrinacia, urges the "black night" (p. 189); Bloom makes for the hospital at ten o'clock. The names Helios and Hyperion—I suggest this likeness only as a verbal echo, which may or may not conceal some significance—seem to be recast in the names of the street, Hollis, and the head of the hospital, Horne. The triple invocation to the latter—"Send us, bright one, light one, Horhorn, quickening and wombfruit" (p. 377) —describes the function of Helios Hyperion precisely.

Odysseus and his men stay their ship in the hollow harbor (p. 190); Bloom comes inside the gate of the hospital (p. 379). Zeus the cloud-gatherer rouses a tempest (p. 190); "Lo, levin leaping lightens in eyeblink Ireland's westward welkin!" (p. 379). After the storm, the Achaeans "beached the ship, and dragged it up within a hollow cave" (p. 190); after the lightning, Bloom "went in Horne's house" (p. 379). However, Odysseus has landed on the island against his better judgment. He adjured the men to drive the ship past the isle, for Teiresias and Circe "very straitly charged me to shun the isle of Helios" (p. 189), a falsehood; [10] when Dixon, Joyce's Eurylochus and representative of the "crew" in the hospital,

> said . . . that he [Bloom] should go into that castle for to make merry with them that were there . . . the travel-ler Leopold said that he should go otherwither [sic] for he was a man of cautels and a subtle. Also the lady . . . trowed well that the traveller had said thing that was false for his subtility [p. 380].

Odysseus yields to the argument of traveller's fatigue; Bloom "went into the castle for to rest him for a space being sore of limb after many marches environing in divers lands . . ." (*ibid.*). Once on the island Odysseus falls asleep, awakening, we may assume, refreshed (pp. 191, 192); "Bloom there for a languor he had but was now better" (p. 391).

The slaughter of cattle is the theme of the Thrinacian episode; the slaughter of cattle is harped upon by the hospital "crew." "*Mort aux vaches*" (p. 392), says one. "What, says Mr Leopold . . . will they slaughter all?" (*ibid.*). And the son of Cronos (*Odyssey*, p. 193) is re-called in the mention of "father Cronion" (*Ulysses*, p. 414).

The brothel scene is allied with Odysseus' sojourn on the isle of Aia by Stephen's use of the name *Circe* (*Ulysses*, p. 493). In keeping with Joyce's treatment of the Sirens, the heavenly Circe is reduced to a bawd and her four hand-maids (*Odyssey*, p. 155) to three whores and a cook. To

Homer's men the singing lady is "a goddess . . . or a woman" (*ibid.*, p. 151); to Joyce's men she is a woman only—the glory hath departed. Circe's invitation (*ibid.*, pp. 151, 154) in Joyce becomes any one of three variations on the following theme:

THE BAWD
[*Her voice whispering huskily.*] Sst! Come here till I tell you. Maidenhead inside. Sst.[11]

Circe's beasts fawn like dogs (*Odyssey*, p. 151); a spaniel slinks after Stephen (growling, to be sure), in the form of a retriever he sniffles about Bloom, in the form of a terrier he follows Bloom and Mrs. Breen, wagging his tail (*Ulysses*, pp. 425, 430, 440). As Odysseus follows his men (p. 152), Bloom follows Stephen (p. 426) to the abode of Circe. Among a number of reminders of the transformed men, the Male Brutes with drugged heads stand out.[12] The progress of Circe's charms is followed closely in Joyce. Her "singing in a sweet voice" (p. 151) becomes a gramophone rearing a battered brazen trunk.[13] The gift of moly (*Odyssey*, p. 153) and its efficacy are paralleled with a difference. Bloom deplores the absence of his talisman (*Ulysses*, p. 517), consequently succumbs to Bello (p. 519), again unlike Odysseus is unmanned (p. 523), but is finally relieved when the spell is broken (p. 540). Odysseus is warned lest Circe make him a "dastard and *unmanned*" (p. 153; italics supplied); with the same word Bello pronounces judgment on Bloom (p. 523). Finally, Odysseus' mission to Hades and back is recalled, again with a difference, in Bello's "I can give you a rare old wine that'll send you skipping to hell and back" (p. 531).

In the older *Eumaeus* (*Odyssey*, pp. 209–58), Telemachus, back from over the sea, helps a beggar who is his royal father returned in rags after ten years of wandering over the world; Odysseus, on his return, was attacked by dogs; Telemachus is unwelcome to the suitors who beset the grass widow of Ithaca; it is twenty years since the outbreak of the Trojan War; Odysseus spins a yarn which is doubted, though it is not pure invention; there is a "false" report that Odysseus is alive. In the younger *Eumaeus*, the *"soi-disant* sailor" (*Ulysses*, p. 614) has a son who ran off to sea (p. 615); Stephen gives a beggar a halfcrown (p. 602); the beggar is an "anything but immaculately attired . . . nobleman" (*ibid.*); the sailor's story about the namesake of Stephen's father "might be a matter of ten years. He toured the wide world . . ." (p. 608); Bloom considers that, "as regards return, you were a lucky dog if they didn't set the terrier at you directly you got back" (p. 634); Stephen is unwelcome to his associates after a row (p. 603); Bloom pictures "a grass widow, at the selfsame fireside. Believes me dead. Rocked in the cradle of the deep" (pp. 608–9), and thinks that "man, or men in the plural, were always hanging around on the waiting list about a lady" (p. 639); land troubles of twenty years ago (p. 613; cf. p. 633) are mentioned; the sailor tells a tall tale which is doubted by Bloom (p. 619) though he believes it is built on a basis of fact; [14] and we hear of false reports that Parnell is alive (p. 633). Against these parallels must be set the fact that Odysseus and Telemachus arrive at the swineherd's separately, while Bloom and Stephen, as a result of the violation of the Homeric pattern which I have noted in connection with *The Oxen of the Sun*, come to the cabman's shelter together.

For the last two episodes of *Ulysses*, the corresponding portions of the *Odyssey*, from Book XVII to the end, seem interlocked, Penelope coming and going at will; I shall therefore consider *Ithaca* and *Penelope* jointly. Of the content of this section of Joyce, Gilbert writes:

> It is, however, significant that Joyce, characteristically averse from scenes of carnage, compresses his counterpart for the section of Homer's Odyssey (a quarter of the entire poem) which deals with the slaughter of the suitors, into a single episode (less than a tenth of *Ulysses*). [p. 346, n. 1; cf. also Budgen, p. 256.]

Earlier in the book, Gilbert stated that "*Ulysses* achieves a coherent and integral interpretation of life, a static beauty according to the definition of Aquinas: *ad pulchri-tudinem tria requiruntur integritas, consonantia, claritas*" (p. 8). In a footnote Gilbert refers to the source of this quotation in the *Portrait*, where Stephen holds that "the esthetic emotion . . . is . . . static" (p. 240) and that in proper art "the artist, like the God of the creation, remains within or behind or beyond or above his handiwork, invisible, refined out of existence, indifferent, paring his fingernails" (p. 252). "The feelings excited by improper art are kinetic, desire or loathing" (p. 240). In view of these passages and Gilbert's note, Joyce, it seems to me, would be hard put to it to defend himself for permitting his temperamental bent to determine the character of the Homeric parallel.

Of direct correspondences the final episodes yield a few. Telemachus tells his mother that Menelaus, hearing of the activities of the suitors, said: "Out upon them, for truly in the bed of a brave-hearted man were they minded to lie" (*Odyssey*, p. 263); Bloom might say more, they have lain. Odysseus, the "beggar" who looks back to his former wealth, is recalled in Bloom's ambition to construct a sumptuous villa (*Ulysses*, pp. 697–701) and in his subsequent, likewise hypothetical impoverishment (p. 710). Both Odysseus and Bloom have a long list of travelling companions, Bloom's (p. 722) a comic counterpart of Odysseus'. And of both it may be said: "He rests. He has travelled" (*Ulysses, ibid.*).

Finally, Molly Bloom's reverie appears to take its roots in the experience of Penelope. "While sleep laid hold of him [Odysseus] loosening the cares of his soul . . . his good wife awoke . . . to Artemis first the fair lady made her prayer" (pp. 312–13). And in the prayer we are given a modest foretaste of Molly Bloom: "For furthermore this very night one seemed to lie by my side, in the likeness of my lord . . . and then was my heart glad. . . ." [1]

IN *From the Old Waterford House*, a book that is virtu-
ally unknown in this country [1] although it contains a
chapter on Joyce that adds significantly to our understanding of his art, Arthur Power, an Irish acquaintance of
Joyce's, reports:

> As for the sources of his inspiration, I remember when
> talking to him one day in Fouquets, on the Champs
> Elysees, of my uncertainty on what creative lines to
> proceed on in regard to writing amid all the confused, and
> it seemed to me, jarring claims of modernity, he recom-
> mended me to study "The Book of Kells."
>
> "In all the places I have been to, Rome, Geneva,
> Trieste, I have taken it about with me, and gone to it for
> inspiration, poring over its workmanship for hours. It is the
> most purely Irish thing we have, and some of the big
> initial letters which swing right across a page have the
> essential quality of a chapter of 'Ulysses.' Indeed you can
> compare much of my work to the intricate illuminations.
> Study it and see what it can give you, for it, more than
> anything else, is the fountainhead of Irish inspiration.
> . . ." [p. 67]

The key words in this passage, for my purpose, are "intricate illuminations" and "Irish inspiration." *The Book of
Kells* is only one part of the Irish background of *Ulysses*.

By "local allusions" I mean allusions which, like *The
Book of Kells*, might be among the associations of the
Irish mind and would probably not be among the associa-

tions of the non-Irish mind. My observations concern a work in which the importance of the milieu is common knowledge, though the milieu itself with its myriad details is not so commonly known. I propose to deal with a few of the details which, so far as I have been able to determine, have not yet been elucidated.

In the funeral scene, Simon Dedalus, who is a native of Cork, asks Ned Lambert, who has recently been there: "How are all in Cork's own town?" [2] The question takes on a new dimension when we become aware that, in an Irish mind, "Cork's own town" refers to a popular song of that title,[3] with a history of more than a century and a quarter—a song in which a native of Cork celebrates the city. To convey some impression of the quality of the association in the mind of Simon Dedalus and very likely in the mind of Ned Lambert, I shall cite the first two stanzas:

> *They may rail at the city where first I was born,*
>   *But it's there they've the whiskey, and butter, and pork;*
> *And a neat little spot for to walk in each morn—*
>   *They call it Daunt's Square, and the City is Cork.*
> *The square has two sides—why, one east and one west,*
>   *And convenient's the region of frolic and spree,*
> *Where salmons, drisheens, and beefsteaks are cooked best:*
>   *Och! Fishamble's the Eden for you, love, and me!*
>
> *If you want to behold the sublime and the beauteous,*
>   *Put your toes in your brogues and see sweet Blarney*
>   *Lane,*
> *Where the parents and childer are comely and duteous,*
>   *And dry lodging both rider and beast entertain;*
> *In the cellars below dine the slashing young fellows*
>   *That come with the butter from distant Tralee;*
> *While the landlady, chalking the score on the bellows,*
>   *Sings, Cork is an Eden for you, love, and me!*

In the newspaper-office scene, J. J. O'Molloy says to Myles Crawford, the editor, who has just paid tribute to a Corkman (p. 135): "I hold no brief, as at present advised, for the third profession *qua* profession but your Cork legs

are running away with you" (p. 137). Again, the concluding phrase yields its total meaning only when we are
aware that O'Molloy is probably alluding to the following
ballad, entitled "The Cork Leg":

I'll tell you a story that is no sham,
In Holland there lived a merchant man,
Who every morning said, I am
The richest merchant in Amsterdam.

One day he sat, full as an egg,
When a poor relation came in to beg;
And kicking him out, he kicked a keg,
And kicking this keg he broke his leg.

He told his friends how he was put
About by a friend that he lost a foot,
And says he: "On crutches I'll never walk
For I'll have a beautiful leg of cork."

A doctor came on his vocation
And to him made a long oration,
And at the end of this occupation
He finished all up with an amputation.

When the leg was on, and finished right,
When the leg was on, they screwed it tight,
And although he went with a bit of a hop,
When he grounded the leg it wouldn't stop.

O'er hedges and ditches he scoured the plain,
And to rest his leg he was very fain,
And he threw himself down, but 'twas all in vain,
For the leg pulled him up and was off again.

He called to them that were in sight:
"Oh, stop me, or I am punctured quite!!"
But although their aid he would thus invite,
In less than a second he was out of sight.

And so he kept running from place to place,
And the people thought he was running a race,
And he clung to a post for to stop the pace
But the leg it still kept up the chase.

O'er hedges and ditches he runs full sore,
And Europe he has travelled it o'er,
And although he's dead and is no more,
The leg goes on as it did of yore.

So often you'll see in the dim half light
A merchant man and a cork leg tight,
And from these you may learn that it's wrong to slight
A poor relation with a keg in sight! [4]

In the episode concerning the chauvinistic citizen, the nameless narrator introduces this character and a dog in the following words:

> So we turned into Barney Kiernan's and there sure enough was the citizen up in the corner having a great confab with himself and that bloody mangy mongrel, Garryowen . . .
> The bloody mongrel let a grouse out of him would give you the creeps. Be a corporal work of mercy if someone would take the life of that bloody dog. I'm told for a fact he ate a good part of the breeches off a constabulary man in Santry that came round one time with a blue paper about a license. [p. 290]

A little later, we hear:

> Someone that has nothing better to do ought to write a letter *pro bono publico* to the papers about the muzzling order for a dog the like of that. Growling and grousing and his eye all bloodshot from the drouth is in it and the hydrophobia dropping out of his jaws. [p. 306]

Joyce's point in calling the mangy, vicious mongrel Garryowen becomes fully clear only when we consider that the name fittingly combines the title of a popular Irish roistering song—to go with the nationalist context—and the filthy [5] associations of Garryowen, the suburb of Limerick which the song celebrates. The atmosphere of this song is indicated by the opening stanzas:

> *Let Bacchus's sons be not dismayed,*
> *But join with me each jovial blade;*
> *Come booze and sing, and lend your aid*
> *To help me with the chorus:—*

> *Instead of Spa we'll drink brown ale,*
> *And pay the reckoning on the nail,*
> *No man for debt shall go to gaol*
>   *From Garryowen in glory!*
>
> *We are the boys that take delight in*
> *Smashing the Limerick lamps when lighting,*
> *Through the streets like sporters fighting,*
>   *And tearing all before us.*
>   *Instead, &c.*
>
> *We'll break windows, we'll break doors,*
> *The watch knock down by threes and fours;*
> *Then let the doctors work their cures,*
>   *And tinker up our bruises.*
>   *Instead, &c.*[6]

It is all the more amusing, then, for Joyce later to refer, in parody, to "the really marvellous exhibition of cynanthropy given by the famous old Irish red wolfdog setter formerly known by the *sobriquet* of Garryowen" [7] and, later still, to "grandpapa Giltrap's lovely dog Garryowen that almost talked, it was so human." [8]

In the Swiftian tale of Farmer Nicholas and his bull, in the hospital scene, Dixon, the narrator, says (p. 394): "But one evening . . . when the lord Harry [i.e., Henry VIII] was cleaning his royal pelt to go to dinner after winning a boatrace . . . he discovered in himself a wonderful likeness to a bull . . ." The phrase "royal pelt," it seems to me, might very well recall to some Irish minds a Dublin street ballad which William Butler Yeats recorded before the turn of the century in *The Celtic Twilight*. Michael Moran, "The Last Gleeman," [9] Yeats tells us, had

a poem of his own called *Moses*, which went a little nearer poetry [than did his poem "St. Mary of Egypt"] without going very near. But he could ill brook solemnity, and before long parodied his own verses in the following ragamuffin fashion:

In Egypt's land, contagious to the Nile,
King Pharaoh's daughter went to bathe in style.
She tuk her dip, then walked unto the land,
To dry her royal pelt she ran along the strand.
A bulrush tripped her, whereupon she saw
A smiling babby in a wad o' straw
She tuk it up, and said with accents mild,
' 'Tare-and-agers, girls, which av yez owns the child?'

It is worth noting that, whereas in Moran the phrase "royal pelt" is only humorous, in Joyce it adds up to something more, blending humor with precision as it is applied to the lord Harry at the moment when "he discovered in himself a wonderful likeness to a bull and on picking up a blackthumbed chapbook that he kept in the pantry he found sure enough that he was a lefthanded descendant of the famous champion bull of the Romans, *Bos Bovum*, which is good bog Latin for boss of the show."

For last place I have reserved a piece of elucidation which I do not owe to a published source, though, I might add, borrowing a Joycean phrase, it's sad and weary I was at the end of a long, futile search through various publications. Toward the close of the newspaper-office scene, Stephen Dedalus tells his tale of the two poor, old women who, taking along some brawn and bread and plums, climb to the top of Nelson's Pillar to see the sights of Dublin. Myles Crawford comments: "Out for the waxies' Dargle" (p. 146). In this connection Stuart Gilbert, in the first edition of his authoritative book on *Ulysses*, observed:

> All the action of *Ulysses* takes place in or about the city of Dublin—the unity of place is as thoroughgoing as that of time—and there are many topical allusions to characteristic sights of Dublin streets, to facts and personalities of the Dublin milieu of a quarter of a century ago, that are incomprehensible for most English and American readers and may become so, in course of time, even to Dubliners. But without such 'personal touches,' these nuances of evanescent 'local colour,' the realism of the 'silent monologues' would have been impaired; their presence in *Ulysses* was indispensable. [p. 16]

As a footnote to the phrase "evanescent 'local colour' "
Gilbert added: "Such as the allusions to 'Elvery's elephant
house,' the 'waxies' Dargle,' the 'Old Woman of Prince's
Street' and, generally, to the 'Dublin Castle' *régime*." His
failure to explain the "waxies' Dargle" made him, to my
mind, easily the peer of Thomas Speght, author of what
"has often been called the most exasperating note ever
written on Chaucer." [10] Speght, in 1598, made the following comment on the phrase "Wades boot": "Concerning
Wade and his bote called Guingelot, as also his strange
exploits in the same, because the matter is long and
fabulous, I passe it over." Fortunately, Mr. Gilbert, unlike Speght these three and a half ignorant centuries, is
still amenable to questioning, and on 29 April 1951 he
very kindly made this reply to an inquiry:

> It's so long since Joyce explained to me the meaning of the
> 'waxies' Dargle' that I can't *absolutely* guarantee the
> correctness of what follows—but I'm pretty sure it's right.
>   'The Dargle' is a long glen near Bray (12 miles from
> Dublin) through which the river Dargle flows. (It's men-
> tioned again in 'Ithaca.') According to Black's guide it is
> about a mile long and flanked by a wall of rocks 'beauti-
> fully clothed with native wild wood and graceful fern.'
> (Mr Black can *wax* quite lyrical on occasion!) It is a great
> place for picnics. The 'waxies' had a sort of (annual?)
> fête-day there. What are the 'waxies'? I'm fairly sure that
> Joyce told me they were the cobblers (the appropriateness
> of the name is obvious). To check this I have looked up
> the French edition; we were careful to see we had got the
> meaning right when translating. The words there are
> 'Pour [sic] fêter le [sic] Saint Crépin.' Saint Crépin (i.e.,
> St Crispin q.v.) is the patron saint of cobblers. 'Saint-
> crépin' is used as an equivalent of 'shoemakers' tools.'[11]

It may be worth mentioning that Gilbert in his "second
edition, revised," [12] published a year after the writing of
this letter, made no change in the note in which he had
listed "waxies' Dargle" as a specimen of evanescent local
color.

It is now forty-two years since the publication of *Ulysses*.

The time of its action is sixty years behind us. As a stream-of-consciousness novel, the book is shot through with memories, and memories of memories, which reach back increasing distances into the fading past. It seems to me that we who are now closer to the twenty-first century than to the nineteenth should be well advised to rescue from oblivion as much as possible of the peculiarly Irish milieu of *Ulysses*. What should we not give for the illumination of comparable passages in the Bible, the classics, Dante, or Shakespeare, not to mention again the author of the allusion to Wade's boat?

5 THE CHARACTERIZATION OF STEPHEN DEDALUS IN ULYSSES

THIS ESSAY is a chapter from a longer study, the purpose of which is to analyze the technique of *Ulysses* as it is revealed by the growth of the text through the innumerable, extensive, and significant changes which the author made in various stages in the writing of the book. As the materials of *Ulysses* were going through the creative process in now widely scattered manuscripts, typescripts, proof sheets, and other preliminary drafts, the revisions added up to an enormous body of evidence which yields much new light on Joyce's intentions and methods.

This study takes account of such things as the manuscript notebooks and sheets in the University of Buffalo Library and the Cornell University Library, the manuscript of *Ulysses* in the Rosenbach Foundation, a certain number of the scattered typescript sheets, the partial and untrustworthy serial version in the *Little Review*, a large collection of proof sheets in the Harvard University Library, several proof sheets in the Yale University Library, and other documents in private hands. The fact that the proofs in the Harvard Library alone offer from one to eight galleys for any given segment of *Ulysses* should indicate how the materials afford a fascinating insight into Joyce's methods as well as a basis for observations on the entire history of the evolution of the novel.

The present essay is the first of four chapters on characterization, the second dealing with Leopold Bloom, the third with minor characters, and the fourth with Molly Bloom. (A summary of the second appeared as "The Characterization of Leopold Bloom" in *Literature and Psychology*, IX [Winter, 1959], 3–4; the fourth is reprinted below.)

So far as characterization generally is concerned, Joyce's recorded remarks encourage one to believe that he started with large and fluid concepts which he then proceeded to particularize by concrete, detailed illustration. The reader's experience, however, is inductive, and only after building up a character bit by bit can he perceive the pattern of the whole. More importantly, working from the preliminary versions, he begins at a stage that is inductive for both author and reader, the author introducing details, the reader following the author, both building toward the whole, the first from preconceived outlines, the second toward outlines that are yet to be apprehended. Painstakingly, indefatigably, Joyce linked together the innumerable atoms that finally emerge as Stephen Dedalus, Leopold Bloom, the minor characters, and Molly Bloom. With the benefit of hindsight the reader of the published text may fluently formulate these people as products of this, that, and other forces; the process of creation, however, is recaptured only when he retraces the steps which Joyce took in shaping his characters.

ii

At the time the eighth episode of *Ulysses* was appearing in serial form,[1] Joyce said to Budgen: "I have just got a letter asking me why I don't give Bloom a rest. The writer of it wants more Stephen. But Stephen no longer interests me to the same extent. He has a shape that can't be changed."[2] In this statement lies the key to the way Joyce handled Stephen in the process of revision.

The task before Joyce in dealing with this character was one of continuation rather than creation, and evidence of his skill in the performance is plentiful. Many passages in *Ulysses*, some in essentially the same form, some transmuted, recall directly the Stephen of the *Portrait of the Artist as a Young Man.*

The Stephen who, when Haines expresses the intention of making a collection of his sayings, asks: "—Would I make money by it?" [3] is still the impecunious, embittered Stephen who, when invited to sign a testimonial for universal peace, asked: "—Will you pay me anything if I sign?" [4]

The shy, anti-social Stephen of the *Portrait* also appears in *Ulysses:* imagined experiences in both works, though outwardly different, prove him one and the same. In the *Portrait,* upon reading the word *Foetus* carved on a desk, Stephen is startled and seems "to feel the absent students of the college about him and *to shrink from their company.*" [5] In *Ulysses,* by the seashore, Stephen thinks back to his Viking ancestors:

> Their blood is in me, their lusts my waves. I moved among them on the frozen Liffey, that I, a changeling, among the spluttering resin fires. *I spoke to no-one; none to me.*[6]

The shyness and aloofness are deep-rooted. One of Stephen's earliest memories, in the *Portrait,* is of hiding under the table when the Vances visit.[7] And not much later, though the record dates much later, he is "reluctant to give his hand in salutation" to Leopold Bloom.[8]

Stephen is consistent in the cast of his thought. An entry in the diary which concludes the earlier tale, reads in part:

> This confused her more and I felt sorry and mean. Turned off that valve at once and opened the spiritual-heroic refrigerating apparatus, invented and patented in all countries by Dante Alighieri. Talked rapidly of myself and my plans.[9]

The same cold mocking jocosity pervades the following from *Ulysses:*

> Seadeath, mildest of all deaths known to man. Old Father Ocean. *Prix de Paris*: beware of imitations. Just you give it a fair trial. We enjoyed ourselves immensely.[10]

The profound influence of the Church upon him is reflected in both works not only in his theological pre-occupations but also in the sacerdotal images by which his mind is objectified for us.[11] The Church, even after he has rejected it, dominates his thought. As his friend Cranly put it, 'his mind is supersaturated with the religion in which he says be disbelieves.'[12] And Stephen himself, while employing the scholastic method, asks: "Are you condemned to do this?"[13] When, therefore, at the opening of *Ulysses*, Mulligan addresses Stephen as a "fearful jesuit";[14] when, in the brothel scene, one of the whores is sure that Stephen is a spoiled priest or a monk;[15] and when, in the mad whirl of that episode, he is elevated to the primacy of all Ireland,[16] we understand, for all such passages have a center of reference in the earlier portrait.

Similarly, "Aquinas tunbelly"[17] and his "gorbellied works"[18] come recognizably from the young man who some six months before said: "Now, we can return to our old friend saint Thomas for another pennyworth of wisdom."[19]

However, we are dealing not merely with consistency in broad outline, in the presentation of patent aspects of personal history, thought, and language, but also with consistency in the very images and metaphors toward which the character inclines in articulating experience, in the peculiar weave of the individual mind. For example, Stephen, in the *Portrait*, extremely sensitive to words, murmurs the phrase "A day of dappled seaborne clouds":

> The phrase and the day and the scene harmonized in a chord. Words. Was it their colours? He allowed them to glow and fade, hue after hue: sunrise gold, the russet and green of apple orchards, azure of waves, the greyfringed fleece of clouds. No, it was not their colours: it was the poise and balance of the period itself. Did he then love the rhythmic rise and fall of words better than their associations of legend and colour? Or was it that, being as weak of sight as he was shy of mind, he drew less pleasure from the reflection of the glowing sensible world through the prism of a language manycoloured and richly storied

than from the contemplation of an inner world of individual emotions mirrored perfectly in a lucid supple
periodic prose.[20]

In the cabman's shelter, in *Ulysses*, Stephen makes the
same transfer between the senses of sound and sight:

> He could hear, of course, all kinds of words changing
> colour like those crabs about Ringsend in the morning,
> burrowing quickly into all colours of different sorts of the
> same sand where they had a home somewhere beneath or
> seemed to.[21]

In addition to such unity in texture of thought, Stephen
carries over from the *Portrait* memories the full meaning
of which for Stephen the reader cannot possibly arrive at
without recourse to the earlier work. For example, in Mr.
Deasy's schoolhouse, while helping a weak, unprepossess-
ing pupil, he thinks:

> Yet someone had loved him, borne him in her arms and
> in her heart. . . . She had loved his weak watery blood
> drained from her own. Was that then real? The only true
> thing in life? [22]

In the library, discoursing on Shakespeare, he remarks:
"*Amor matris*, subjective and objective genitive, may be
the only true thing in life." [23] And in the brothel his
mother, objectifying his imagination, says: "Years and
years I loved you, O my son, my firstborn, when you lay in
my womb." [24] None of these passages yields its full measure of meaning without the memory of Cranly's speech to
Stephen in the *Portrait*:

> —Whatever else is unsure in this stinking dunghill of a
> world a mother's love is not. Your mother brings you into
> the world, carries you first in her body. What do we know
> about what she feels? But whatever she feels, it, at least,
> must be real. It must be.[25]

In the newspaper office we hear:

> —I want you to write something for me, he [Crawford]
> said. Something with a bite in it. You can do it. I see it in
> your face. *In the lexicon of youth. . .*

See it in your face. See it in your eye. Lazy idle little schemer.[26]

The reader who is mystified by the second paragraph, must wait until the brothel scene for some, though still inadequate, elaboration. There, Stephen, bringing a match near his eye in the attempt to light a cigarette, says: "Must get glasses. Broke them yesterday. Sixteen years ago." [27] Shortly afterward Lynch's use of the word *pandybat* precipitates the hallucination of Father Dolan of Clongowes, who repeats himself substantially as of the *Portrait*: "Any boy want flogging? Broke his glasses? Lazy idle little schemer. See it in your eye." [28] And once more the rector, Father Conmee, comes to Stephen's aid.

In his use of Shelley's comparison of the mind in creation to a fading coal,[29] Stephen repeats briefly a loan to which, in the *Portrait*, he gave a place of climactic significance.[30] And not only the consistency of the character, but also the identity of character and creator is reinforced when one discovers that Joyce himself borrowed the same image in his early essay on Mangan,[31] before the *Portrait* was begotten or *Ulysses* conceived.

When John Eglinton comments on the strangeness of Stephen's surname, the young man thinks:

Fabulous artificer, the hawklike man. You flew. Whereto? Newhaven-Dieppe, steerage passenger. Paris and back. Lapwing. Icarus. *Pater, ait.* Seabedabbled, fallen, weltering. Lapwing you are. Lapwing he.[32]

Again, the point of the whole thought becomes clear only when the reader remembers Stephen's vision, in the *Portrait*,[33] of the artificer of old whose name he bears.

As Stephen passes through the portico of the library, he thinks: "Here I watched the birds for augury. Ængus of the birds. They go, they come." [34]—still another memory from the *Portrait*.[35]

Such memories continued without explanation may be justified, as I have written elsewhere, on the ground that, since Stephen is in what, regarding his character, is a sequence of two novels, the reader may be expected to know the first novel before beginning the second. The justification would, however, be tantamount to an admission that, as regards Stephen, *Ulysses* does not constitute an artistic whole. Bloom, also, has his memories—but with a difference. During the lunch hour, for instance, his mind runs on the slaughter of animals:

> Wretched brutes there at the cattlemarket waiting for the poleaxe to split their skulls open. Moo. Poor trembling calves. Meh. Staggering bob. Bubble and squeak. Butcher's buckets wobble lights. Give us that brisket off the hook. Plup. Rawhead and bloody bones. Flayed glasseyed sheep hung from their haunches, sheepsnouts bloodypapered snivelling nosejam on sawdust. Top and lashers going out. Don't maul them pieces, young one.[36]

Who is it that gives the orders in this sequence of thoughts? Bloom's former employer at the cattlemarket, Mr. Cuffe. If we have not learned much about Bloom's experience with Cuffe from the one mention of the latter up to this point,[37] we are destined to glean the whole story from a number of succeeding allusions—within *Ulysses*.[38]

But Joyce goes even further, and the reader who has familiarized himself with the *Portrait* in preparation for *Ulysses* meets the following, in the third episode: "Remember your epiphanies on green oval leaves, deeply deep, copies to be sent if you died to all the great libraries of the world, including Alexandria?"[39] Again, in the library scene, he meets: "Where is your brother? Apothecaries' hall. My whetstone. Him, then Cranly, Mulligan: now these. Speech, speech."[40] And in the brothel scene he hears Stephen call Lynch's cap "Whetstone!"[41] He combs the *Portrait* for explanation in vain. Gradually, perhaps, a meaning of a sort patches itself together for the "whetstone" passages, but the epiphanies remain opaque. The fact is that Stephen is leaning upon discussions of both epiphanies and whetstones in the early manuscript draft of the *Portrait* a portion of which was published posthumously as *Stephen Hero*, a manuscript which Joyce himself did not intend to publish;[42] and for the epiphanies, further, upon a series of notes, also published posthumously.[43] Perhaps it may be urged that blind spots occupy a legitimate place in one's understanding of another mind. But since explanations for these particular spots did exist, surely blindness here is an unnecessary affliction.

With Stephen so fully realized in advance of *Ulysses* that Joyce even trails over loose ends from manuscripts, it is understandable that the revisions relating to this character, while illuminating, should not be numerous.

Stephen's congenital shyness transpires when, in reciting his *Parable of the Plums*, he first thinks: "On now. Let there be life."—then, with an addition in proof: "On now. Dare it. Let there be life." [44] His pride asserts itself inwardly in the library. He thinks: "They make him [Mulligan] welcome." Following this, Joyce adds: "*Was Du verlachst wirst Du noch dienen.*" [45]

Shyness, pride, and exacerbation at being undervalued, resulting in a cold, isolated intellectualism, strengthen Stephen's inclination to mockery. The "born sneerer" of the *Portrait* [46] reminds Professor MacHugh "of Antisthenes, . . . a disciple of Gorgias, the sophist. It is said of him that none could tell if he were bitterer against others or against himself." [47] Amid comrades who drool journalese, Stephen offers to stand drinks: "—Gentlemen, Stephen said. May I suggest that the house do now adjourn?" But Joyce has not yet done with the mind of his character, and, by an addition in proof, Stephen assumes mockingly and completely the banality of his companions: "—Gentlemen, Stephen said. As the next motion on the agenda paper may I suggest that the house do now adjourn?" [48]

In the brothel, Stephen takes up a slightly fuddled version of the riddle with which he mystified his morning class:

> The fox crew, the cocks flew
> The bells in heaven
> Were striking eleven
> 'Tis time for her poor soul
> To go to heaven.

But, remembering perhaps that Stephen is now free from the constraint of the schoolhouse, Joyce gives the sneerer in him free rein: for "go to" he substitutes "get out of", adding a gibe against the theology which Stephen has repudiated.[49]

Joyce gives Stephen another opportunity to scoff at the Church. Stephen has just uttered one of his sententious pronouncements upon his significance, and the impersonal catechism of *Ithaca* continues:

> Was this affirmation apprehended by Bloom?
> Not verbally. Substantially.

> What spectacle confronted them when they, first the host, then the guest, emerged silently, doubly dark, from obscurity by a passage from the rere of the house into the penumbra of the garden?
> The heaventree of stars hung with humid nightblue fruit.

Between the two pairs of question and answer Joyce adds a brace of new ones:

> In what order of precedence, with what attendant ceremony was the exodus from the house of bondage to the wilderness of inhabitation effected?

> Lighted Candle in Stick
> borne by
> *Bloom*
> Diaconal Hat on Ashplant
> borne by
> STEPHEN

> With what intonation *secreto* of what commemorative psalm?
> The 57th, *modus peregrinus*: *In exitu Israel de Egypto*: *domus David de populo barbaro*.[50]

When we consider the muddle that is Bloom's half-educated mind, there can be little doubt that the intoner is Stephen.

Like many an inartistic young man, the shy and proud mocker fortifies his self-esteem with an erudition that often degenerates into pedantry. At one point in the library scene, the talk is of Shakespeare's second-best bed:

> —Antiquity mentions famous beds, John Eglinton puckered, bedsmiling, [sic] Let me think.
> —Do you mean he died so? Mr Best asked with concern. I mean. . .

Between these paragraphs Joyce adds in proof:

> —That Stagyrite school urchin, Stephen said, who when dying in exile frees and endows his slaves, pays tribute to his elders, wills to be laid in earth near the bones of his wife and bids his friends be kind to an old mistress (don't forget Nell Gwynn Herpyllis) and let her live in his villa.

Then, in the addition, before "wife" Joyce adds a touch of preciosity in "dead".[51] In the next galley, after "school-urchin" [sic], Joyce adds "and heathen sage", then before "heathen" the pedantic circumstance "bald".[52]

After Bloom chants the opening lines of *Ha-Tikvah* to Stephen and the latter signs his name in Irish and Roman characters, we read:

> What was Bloom's visual sensation?
> He saw in a quick young male familiar form the predestination of the future.
>
> What future careers had been possible for him in the past and with what exemplars?

Dividing the answer from the question to which it gives rise by the verbal link ("future"), Joyce inserts:

> What were Stephen's and Bloom's quasisimultaneous volitional quasisensations?
> Visually, Stephen's: The traditional figure of hypostasis, depicted by Johannes Damascenus, Lentulus Romanus and Epiphanius Monachus as leucodermic, sesquipedalian with winedark hair.
> Auditively, Bloom's: [53]

Stephen's most tiresome display of learning comes in the discussion of Shakespeare, which he converts into an opportunity to muster, with the tediousness of an antiquarian, a thousand and one gratuitous details relating to Shakespeare's experience and background. His prodigal minuteness, though it springs largely from the ostentatious impulse,[54] probably owes a great deal also to his habit of recording to the last detail his observations as potential artist. The kinship of creator with character in this regard is notable in such scenes as the feeding of the cat [55] and, on a larger scale, the funeral,[56] in which ordinary experience, infinitesimally rendered, takes on a living glow. The difference between Stephen in the library and Joyce in these scenes, is the difference between apprentice and master.

The unfledged artist, still too young to contain his knowledge, often regurgitates. His performance in the library is foreshadowed early in the day, when Haines asks him to state his Hamlet theory and Mulligan interposes:

> —No, no, Buck Mulligan shouted in pain. I'm not equal to Thomas Aquinas and the fifty-five reasons he has made to prop it up. Wait till I have a few pints in me first.[57]

In the discussion itself, after an initiatory "—Saint Thomas" of Stephen's is cut off by an *"Ora pro nobis"* and a ribald keen from Mulligan, we hear:

> —Saint Thomas, Stephen, smiling, said, writing of incest from a stand point [sic] different from that of the Viennese school Mr. Magee spoke of, likens it in his wise and curious way to an avarice of the emotions.

After "said," Joyce adds "whose works I enjoy reading in the original,".[58]

Stephen's next long speech first reads in part:

> In old age she takes up with gospellers (one stayed at New Place and drank a quart of sack the town paid for but in which bed he slept it skills not to ask) and heard she had a soul. Venus has twisted her lips in prayer.

Between these sentences Joyce adds:

> She read or had read to her his chapbooks preferring them to the *Merry Wives* and thought over *Hooks and Eyes for Believers' Breeches* and *The Most Spiritual Snuffbox to make* [sic] *the Most Devout Souls Sneeze* [sic] [59]

The discussion at the lying-in hospital, again, offers both author and character many opportunities for parading the recondite. In a manuscript notebook, the sentence "Then spake young Stephen of holy church, of law of canons, of birth by wind, or divers fable." becomes "Then spake young Stephen, orgulous, of mother church, of law of canons, of bigness wrought by wind of seeds of brightness and demons, or divers fable." [60] The Rosenbach manuscript reads:

> Then spoke young Stephen orgulous of mother Church that would cast him from her bosom, of law of canons, of bigness wrought by wind of seeds of brightness or by potency of vampires mouth to mouth or, as Virgilius saith, by the influence of the occident or peradventure in her bath according to the opinions of Averroes and Moses Maimonides.

With minor variations, this is the version in proof, in which before "peradventure" Joyce adds "by the reek of moonflower or an she lie with a woman which her man has but lain with, *effectu secuto*,". [61]

The discussion moves on:

> Thereat mirth grew in them the more and they rehearsed to him [Stephen] his curious rite of wedlock for the disrobing and deflowering of spouses, she to be in guise of white and saffron, her groom in white and grain, with burning of nard and tapers, on a bribered while clerks sung kyries and the anthem *Ut novetur sexus omnis corporis mysterium* till she was there unmaided.

But the esoteric origin of Stephen's ceremony is hinted at only in the addition, after "spouses", of ", as the priests use in Madagascar island,". [62] Stephen's curious gleanings here pay him dividends.

Before the episode is out, he capitalizes on his bookish familiarity with nautical jargon. The Swiftian fable of Farmer Nicholas' bull is drawing to a close, in manuscript:

> They were, says Mr Stephen, and the end was that the men of the island seeing no help was toward, as the

> ungrate women were all of one mind, made a wherry raft, loaded themselves and their bundles of chattels on shipboard, set all masts erect, sprang their luff, set her head on between wind and water, let the bullgine run ran up the jolly Roger and pushed off to recover the main of America.

After "jolly Roger" Joyce adds "weighed her anchor". In proof, the end of the sentence has become:

> set all masts erect, manned the yards, sprang their luff, heaved to, spread three sheets in the wind, put her head between wind and water, weighed anchor, ported her helm, ran up the jolly Roger, gave three times three and let the bullgine run and pushed off in their bumboat to recover the main of America.

And, as if to insure the exhaustion of Stephen's repertory, Joyce alters the conclusion of the passage to read: "gave three times three, let the bullgine run [*sic*] pushed off in their bumboat and put to sea to recover the main of America." [63]

Even the intoxication and fatigue of the evening in nighttown do not obliterate Stephen's learning; if anything, by relaxing censorship, they encourage his inclination to display it. In the cabman's shelter, Bloom has just suggested that Parnell's paramour was Spanish:

> —The king of Spain's daughter, Stephen answered.
> —Was she? Bloom said, surprised, though not astonished by any means.

After "answered" Joyce appends:

> , adding something about farewell and adieu to you Spanish onions and the first land called the Deadman and from Ramhead to Scilly was so and so many. . .

Then, after "something" Joyce inserts, appropriately, "or other rather muddled".[64] Though Stephen perpetrates the "Spanish onions" wilfully, he unwittingly confuses, in his present state, the lines of an old capstan chanty entitled "Spanish Ladies." [65]

Much of Stephen's knowledge, as we have already seen, reflects his ecclesiastical training. The effect of this influence, too, upon his thinking is gradually and surely built up in the process of revision. In the first episode (the art of which is Theology [66]) Stephen, resenting the deference of the old dairywoman to Mulligan, thinks of "her woman's unclean loins." After "loins" Joyce adds ", of man's flesh made not in God's likeness." [67] And following this addition, Joyce later introduced ", the serpent's prey." [68]

In the second episode (the art of which is History [69]), in a passage already cited, Stephen's thoughts turn to mother love: "The only true thing in life?" After this question Joyce adds: "His mother's prostrate body the fiery Columbanus in holy zeal bestrode." [70] Here Joyce is following up the insertion made earlier, in a manuscript notebook containing the third episode, between Stephen's thoughts "You were going to do wonders, weren't you?" and "Pretending to speak broken English", of "Missionary to Europe like the fiery Columbanus." [71] Following this addition, between the Rosenbach manuscript and the Hanley proof, Joyce must have added further: "Fiacre and Scotus on their creepystools in heaven spilt from their pintpots, loudlatinlaughing: *Euge! Euge!*"

In the library Stephen's religious training again contributes to his thought: "Hiesos Kristos, magician of the beautiful. This verily is that." After "beautiful" Joyce adds ", the Logos who suffers at every moment."—then, after "suffers", "in us".[72] Stephen continues: "The Christ with the bridesister, moisture of light, born of a virgin, repentant sophia, departed to the plane of buddhi." Joyce replaces "a" by "an ensouled".[73] In the discussion at the lying-in hospital, Stephen asks: "But what of those Godpossibled souls that we nightly impossibilise?" After "impossibilise" Joyce inserts ", which is the sin against the Holy Ghost, Very God Lord and Giver of Life?" [74]

Theological preoccupations lead Stephen through psychological self-examination into the realm of art.

Chief among Stephen's psychological problems is the relationship between father and son, the issue of his personal experience reverberated by the Christological question on the one hand and the Homeric correspondence on the other. In the library Stephen comments mentally on an observation of Mr. Best's: "Has the wrong sow by the lug." To this thought Joyce adds: "He is in his father. I am in my son." Then he reverses the positions of "his" and "my".[75] Somewhat later Buck Mulligan, whom Stephen secretly regards askance as of the "brood of mockers",[76] overhears Stephen remark on "him who is the substance of his shadow, the son consubstantial with the father"[77] and says to Stephen: "Have you drunk the four quid? Telegram!" Between the question and the exclamation Joyce adds: "The aunt is going to call on your unsubstantial father."[78] Mulligan, in one word, glances at the impecuniosity of the elder Dedalus and derides Stephen's ecclesiastical language as he did earlier his ecclesiastical mind.

The problem of derivation is inseparable from that of identity, and to this question, also, Stephen gives thought. Discussing the Shakespearean mystery of "W. H.," Stephen offers mentally an alternative to the identification with Willie Hughes: "Or Hughie Wills."—following which Joyce adds: "Mr William Himself. W. H: who am I?"[79]

But theology and the mysteries of personality dwindle into insignificance before the overwhelming importance, in Stephen's life, of art. We remember well this side of Stephen from the *Portrait*, the Stephen whose aloofness and detachment and observant manner set him apart for the artist's calling. Temperament, training, and the direction in which the form of the novel was moving, all combined to encourage the development of an art, and a theory of art, which laid primary emphasis upon the impersonal. Experience became for Stephen the stuff of notebooks, and Stephen a cosmological eye. The same detached observation continues in *Ulysses*. Hearing newsboys announce a racing special, Stephen thinks: "Dublin." By the addition, after this, of "I have much, much to learn."[80] Joyce gives us a glimpse into the mind of the artist contemplating the equipment necessary for the work which he has announced for production within ten years.[81] Stephen's next speech is: "—I have a vision too," [82] and his next thought: "Dubliners." [83] In the library, we over-hear the artist garnering impressions: "See this. Remember." [84] As he follows Mulligan out of the library, he quotes his future record: "One day in the national library we had a discussion. Shakes. After his lub back I followed." [85]

His devotion to the objective—again we remember from the *Portrait*—led Stephen to adopt an attitude toward his homeland and its renewed aspirations so fiercely anti-pathetic as to send him into self-imposed exile. During the six months between his flight and his forced return, noth-ing happened to modify his position. Old Gummy Granny appears before him in the brothel:

> [*She wails with banshee woe.*] Ochone! Ochone! Silk of the kine!

STEPHEN

The hat trick!

After "kine!" Joyce adds: "(*she wails*) You met with poor old Ireland and how does she stand?"; [86] and before "The hat trick!": "How do I stand you?" [87] To Bloom, in the cabman's shelter: "—You suspect, Stephen retorted with a sort of laugh, that I may be important because I belong to Ireland." Joyce adds "the *faubourg Saint Patrice* called" before "Ireland" and, after the latter, "for short." [88] On the way to Bloom's house, the pair discuss a number of sub-jects, duly listed. Between "the Roman catholic church," and "jesuit education" Joyce adds ", the Irish nation," [89] juxtaposing religion and nationality, long coupled in the Irish mind and both repudiated by the younger man.

But the detachment of the artist is no more than the setting for Stephen's greatest interest, language. His pas-sion for words, for punning, phrasebuilding, epigram-matizing, modelled of course upon that of his creator, is everywhere evident. Thus, there are accretions in punning and phrasebuilding.

In an addition already cited, Stephen describes Shakespeare's widow in the act of "loosing her nightly waters on the jordan".[90] In keeping with much of the style of the library episode, the pun hinges upon a word (*jordan*) that was current in Shakespeare's time.

The young artist's alertness to the process of language inspires additions. He builds a quatrain at intervals. By the seashore he thinks:

> He comes, pale vampire, through storm his eyes, his bat sails bloodying the sea, mouth to her mouth's kiss.
> Here. Put a pin in that chap, will you? My tablets. Mouth to her kiss. No. Must be two of 'em. Glue 'em well. Mouth to her mouth's kiss.
> His lips lipped and mouthed fleshless lips of air: mouth to her womb. Oomb, allwombing tomb.[91]

In the newspaper office, he has worked out the verses:

> *On swift sail flaming*
> *From storm and south*
> *He comes, pale phantom,*
> *Mouth to my mouth.*

Joyce adds to the consistency and precision of Stephen's thought by changing "*phantom*" to "*vampire*".[92] Somewhat later in the same episode, under the headline "RHYMES AND REASONS", we overhear Stephen again phrase-building:

> Mouth, south. Is the mouth south someway? Or the south a mouth? Must be some. South, pout, out, shout, drouth. Rhymes: two men dressed the same, looking the same, two by two.

> . . . . *la tua pace*
> . . . . *che parlar ti piace*
> . . . . *mentrechè il vento, come fa, si tace.*

> He saw them three by three, approaching girls, in green, in rose, in russet, entwining, *per l'aer perso* in mauve, in purple, *quella pacifica oriafiamma*, in gold or oriflamme, *di rimirar fé più ardenti*. But I old men, penitent, leaden-footed, underdarkneath the night: mouth south: tomb womb.[93]

The last sentence, in proof, reads: "But I old men, penitent, leadenfooted: mouth south: tomb womb." Joyce adds "underdarkneath the night:",[94] further weighting the heavy tread of the "old men" and at the same time introducing into the word-seeking, creative mind of Stephen a modification, by intussusception, of conventional language. We shall witness more modifying presently.

In the discussion at the library Stephen turns a phrase. "—Antisthenes, pupil of Gorgias, Stephen took the palm of beauty from Kyrios Menelaus' broodmare, Argive Helen, and handed it to poor Penelope." Joyce supplies the obvious omission of "said," after "Stephen",[95] and after "Helen," adds "the wooden mare of Troy in whom a score of heroes slept,".[96] Thus, an almost straightforward quotation of Professor MacHugh's earlier speech on the same subject [97] has been converted into a statement that is Stephen's own, marked by the characteristic indentations of his 'literary' bite.

But like his creator, Stephen is not confined to a single language. After his statement in the brothel: "Queens lay with prize bulls." Joyce adds: "Remember Pasiphae for whose lust my grandoldgrossfather made the first confessionbox." [98] To produce the macaronic "grandoldgrossfather", Stephen has welded together English *grandfather*, Gaelic *sean-atair* (literally, 'old-father'), and German *Grossvater*, all three identical in meaning but adding up in their new arrangement to the glancing disparagement of Stephen's eponym, the framer of the wooden cow in which Minos' queen compassed her lust for a bull [99]—the mythical artificer whom, interestingly enough, Stephen had invoked, at the conclusion of the *Portrait*, as his "old father." [100]

6   THE CHARACTERIZATION OF MOLLY BLOOM

This essay, as indicated in the opening section of the preceding essay, is the last of four chapters on characterization, the first dealing with Stephen Dedalus, the second with Leopold Bloom, and the third with minor characters.

LIKE HER HUSBAND, Mrs. Bloom is a new creation in *Ulysses*; and again, in consequence, the various stages in the writing swarm with changes.

About the genesis of Molly, as about that of Bloom, Herbert Gorman gives us authoritative information:

> There were two models for this great character of Molly Bloom, one a Dubliner and the other an Italian. The wartime correspondence of the Italian passed through Joyce's hands during the period he lived in Zurich. There was nothing political in these letters, whose grammar Joyce corrected, but the Austrian censors must have had more than one sizzling moment while reading them. That, however, did not perturb the full-blooded Italian lady.[1]

We shall find that this account, in spite of its brevity, explains much of the character for whom the Italian woman sat.

Again as in the case of her husband, Mrs. Bloom is given no formal descriptive introduction. We grow acquainted with her physical appearance by the same process of accretion which Joyce uses for all his other characters. In view of Molly's effect upon men, it is appropriate that we gain most of our information concerning her physique from the impressions of the men who know her, chief among whom, of course, is her husband. We learn gradually—to cite only a few passages from among a great many—that she has "large soft bubs sloping within her nightdress like a shegoat's udder" and "full lips",[2] large young Moorish eyes inherited with her figure from her Spanish mother,[3] a "plump . . . generous arm," [4] thick wavy black hair,[5] a plump body,[6] ample buttocks,[7] a dark complexion.[8]

The nearest thing to a formal description of Molly comes toward the end of the day and concerns not Molly herself but an approximately eight-year-old photograph of her,

> showing a large sized lady, with her fleshy charms on evidence in an open fashion, as she was in the full bloom of womanhood, in evening dress cut ostentatiously low for the occasion to give a liberal display of bosom, with more than vision of breasts, her full lips parted, and some perfect teeth . . . eyes, dark, large, . . .[9]

For the most part, it will be noted, the likeness still holds.

In revising, Joyce adds to our awareness of several points in Molly's appearance. Thus, Bloom, ordering white wax for her, thinks: "Brings out the darkness of her eyes. Looking at me, the sheet up to her eyes smelling herself, when I was fixing the links in my cuffs." After the second "eyes" Joyce adds ", Spanish,".[10]

At twilight Bloom thinks back upon Cissy Caffrey: "And the dark one with the mop head and the nigger mouth. I knew she could whistle. Mouth made for that." After the last phrase Joyce adds: ". Like Molly." [11] Considering what we know about Molly's appearance, it would have been little wonder had Cissy's complexion or hair, as well as her mouth, inspired the comparison; the three together make it inevitable.

Molly herself remembers

> the day I was in fits of laughing with the giggles I couldn't stop about all my hairpins falling one after another youre

always in great humour she [Josie Powell] said yes because
it grigged her because she knew what it meant

Following "another" Joyce inserts "with the mass of hair
I had".[12]

Looking further back to her Gibraltar days, Molly recalls: "I had everything all to myself then a girl Hester
we used to compare our hair she showed me how to settle
it at the back when I put it up". After "hair" Joyce adds
"mine was thicker than hers".[13]

From Molly's physique it is no far cry to the most
salient aspect of her character—her sexuality. She is, as
Joyce wrote, " 'sane full amoral fertilisable untrustworthy
engaging limited prudent indifferent Weib. "Ich bin das
Fleisch das stets bejaht!" ' " [14] Other qualities only modify
this central fact of her existence.

Towards all things, sex included, Molly maintains a
frank attitude. Again and again she measures things by
their *naturalness*. The imperturbability of the full-
blooded Italian woman was not lost in Joyce's character-
transfusion.

In the process of revision, Molly's emphasis on *naturalness* is augmented. Of her husband she thinks: "but of
course hes not natural". After "natural" Joyce adds "like
the rest of the world".[15]

Molly recalls Leopold's courtship: "sending me that
long strool of a song out of the Huguenots to sing in
French to be more classy O beau pays de la Touraine that
I never even sang once". After "once" Joyce adds "explaining and rigmaroling about religion and persecution
he wont let you enjoy anything naturally".[16]

Almost immediately afterward, Molly observes: "they
ought to make chambers a bit bigger so that a woman
could sit on it properly". For "bit bigger" Joyce substitutes
"natural size".[17]

Later in the same galley as that containing the last addition, Molly thinks about triangles: "her husband found it
out well and if he did can he undo it". For "well" Joyce
substitutes "what they did together well naturally".[18]

The sense of guilt so commonly associated with sex is foreign to Molly even beyond the borders of social convention. She recalls some of Bloom's talk: "who is in your mind now tell me who are you thinking of who is it tell me his name who tell me who the German emperor is it yes imagine Im him think of him can you feel". After "feel" Joyce adds "him trying to make a whore of me what he never will".[19]

Molly's straightforward acceptance of the body moves her to disgust with all mincing and concealment. She considers the books Leopold brings her: "the works of Master Francois somebody supposed to be a priest about a child born out of her ear because her bumgut fell out a nice word for any priest to write". After "write" Joyce adds "and her a——e as if any fool wouldnt know what that meant I hate that pretending of all things".[20]

In the same vein Molly thinks of her adultery: "O much about it if thats all the harm ever we did in this vale of tears God knows its not much". After "not much" Joyce inserts "doesn't everybody only they hide it".[21]

Yet, as a member of society Molly is driven to deceit-by-silence. She considers what she will do in the morning: "Ill see if he has that French letter still in his pocketbook I suppose he thinks I dont know". After "know" Joyce inserts "deceitful men they havent pocket enough for their lies then why should we tell them if its the truth they dont believe you".[22]

Molly's elemental attitude toward sex is again introduced in her thoughts on Stephen: "what is he [Bloom] driving at now". After "now" Joyce adds "showing him my photo its not good of me still I look young in it I wonder he didnt make him a present of it altogether and me too after all why not".[23]

That Molly may be completely natural, Joyce gives ambivalence to her emotion toward men: her sexual avidity is set off by resentment and hostility.

In connection with childbirth she thinks:

and Mina Purefoys husband give us a swing out of your whiskers filling her up with a child or twins once a year as

regular as the clock supposed to be healthy supposing I
risked having another

After "healthy" Joyce adds "not satisfied till they have us
swollen out like elephants or I don't know what".[24]

Feeling that she did not look her best while receiving
Boylan, Molly explains:

> besides scrooching down on me like that all the time with
> his big hipbones he's heavy too with his hairy chest for
> this heat better for him put it into me from behind

After "heat" Joyce adds "always having to lie down for
them".[25]

Again on the subject of Boylan she thinks: "I gave my
eyes that look with my hair a bit loose from the tumbling
and my tongue between my lips up to him Thursday Fri-
day one Saturday two Sunday three O Lord I cant wait till
Monday". After "him", between Molly's report of her
recent desire for this particular male and her expression
of impatience for reunion with him, Joyce inserts "the
savage brute".[26]

Having called to mind the "Aristocrats Masterpiece"
and its illustrations, Molly thinks: "that's the kind of
villainy they're always dreaming about with not another
thing in their empty heads then tea and toast for him and
newlaid eggs". After "him" Joyce adds fuel to Molly's
resentment: "buttered on both sides".[27] At a later stage,
after "heads" he inserts "they ought to get slow poison
the half of them".[28]

Yet Molly can extenuate the treatment men accord
women. About Stephen's nightwandering she thinks: "his
poor mother wouldnt like that if she was alive ruining
himself for life perhaps". After "perhaps" Joyce adds:

> still its a lovely hour so silent I used to love coming home
> after dances the air of the night they have friends they can
> talk to weve none either he wants what he wont get or its
> some woman ready to stick her knife in you I hate that in
> women no wonder they treat us the way they do I suppose
> its all the troubles we have makes us so snappy Im not like
> that [29]

Later, after "do" he inserts "we are a dreadful lot of bitches".[30]

When she is in the affirmative mood, Molly excels in the science of attracting the male. Part of an addition in manuscript reads: "a young boy would like me I'd confuse him a little looking at him".[31] In typescript, after "little" Joyce adds "and make him turn red".[32] In proof, between "little" and "and" he inserts "alone with him if we were let him see my garters the new ones"; and after "looking at him" he adds "seduce him I know what boys feel with that down on their cheek".[33]

Molly also knows what her husband feels. She is considering methods of retaining his attention even in the face of competition: "I know several ways". Following this phrase, in manuscript, Joyce adds a specimen: "touch him with my veil and gloves on going out one kiss then would send them all spinning however alright we'll see then".[34] In proof, between "ways" and "touch" he adds another specimen: "ask him to tuck down the collar of my blouse or".[35] In a later proof, he changes "several" to "plenty of".[36]

But Molly's technique has a history, and we are admitted to a number of pages in the chapter on The Winning of Leopold Bloom. She remembers how she thwarted an attempt at a proposal by Bloom: "only for I put him off letting on I was in a temper with my hands and arms full of pastry flour". After "flour" Joyce adds "in any case I let out too much the night before talking of dreams so I didnt want to let him know more than was good for him".[37]

In connection with one of Molly's amours, Joyce, in typescript, adds the thought "he [Bloom] thinks nothing can happen without him knowing".[38] In proof, after "knowing" he inserts "he hadnt an idea about my mother till we were engaged otherwise hed never have got me so cheap as he did".[39]

Molly recalls, among her readings, "the Shadow of Ashlydyat Mrs Henry Wood Henry Dunbar by that other woman". After "woman" Joyce inserts "I lent him afterwards with Mulveys photo in it so as he see I wasn't without".[40]

We gain further insight into Molly's technique when her thought comes round again to her most recent lover: "I wonder was I too heavy sitting on his knee he was so busy he never felt me easy". After "knee" Joyce adds "when I took off only my blouse and skirt first".[41] Later, after "first" he adds "in the other room".[42] Later still, between "knee" and "when" he inserts "I made him sit on the easychair purposely"; and between "me" and "easy", "I hope my breath was sweet after those kissing comfits".[43]

The last example which I shall offer of additions to Molly's technique occurs in her thoughts on Stephen Dedalus as a possible successor to Boylan: "Ill read and study all I can find so he wont think me stupid". After "find" Joyce adds "or learn a bit by heart if I knew who he likes".[44]

Bound up with Molly's desire to attract the male is an old streak of exhibitionism. In manuscript, Joyce adds a childhood memory: "I'm sure that fellow opposite used to be watching with the lights out in the summer and I in my skin hopping around I used to love myself then stripped at the washstand dabbing and creaming".[45] In proof, after "creaming" he adds further "only when it came to the chamber performance I put out the light too so then there were 2 of us".[46]

Now Molly is considering her program for the projected concert: "Ill sing Winds that blow from the south that he gave after the choirstairs performance". After "performance" Joyce adds "Ill change that lace on my black dress to show off my bubs and Ill yes by God Ill get that big fan mended".[47] In the light of this addition, another becomes amusing. Molly's thought has run on to Fanny M'Coy: "skinny thing with a turn in her eye trying to sing my songs shed want to be born all over again and her old green dress like dabbling on a rainy day". After "dress" Joyce adds "with the lowneck as she cant attract them any other way".[48]

A derived form of exhibitionism inspires two additions. Molly is thinking about Mulvey, her first lover: "Perhaps hes married some girl on the black water I was a bit wild after". Following "black water" Joyce adds "she little knows what I did with her beloved husband before he ever dreamt of her in broad daylight too in the sight of the whole world you might say".[49] Later, after "say" he inserts "they could have put an article about it in the Chronicle".[50]

Concerning the possibility of Stephen as successor to Boylan, in a context recently cited, Molly thinks: "and I can teach him [Stephen] the other part Ill make him feel all over him then hell write about me lover and mistress publicly too with our photographs in the papers when he becomes famous". To insure the full satisfaction of Molly's desire for the advertising of her conquest, Joyce adds "all" before "the papers".[51]

After her person, if not before, the most powerful weapon in a woman's arsenal is her clothing—a fact of which Molly is not unmindful. From the text of one galley we may infer that, when she had removed her blouse and skirt, she came in to Boylan in "a short blue silk petticoat," which Bloom later sees. But Joyce deletes "short", and for "silk petticoat" he substitutes "accordion underskirt of blue silk moirette,".[52] Molly's personal charms now turn out to have been reinforced, not by a plain blue silk undergarment, but by one that is likely to have acted upon Boylan more strikingly. Furthermore, the shortness is not permanently eliminated. A short underskirt would be likely, by flaring, to add fullness to Molly's already sizable buttocks, an effect which would hardly escape the sexological technician in Molly—and didn't. For Joyce merely postpones this part of his description of the underskirt to Molly's memory of Boylan's behavior: "no thats no way for him has he no manners . . . slapping us behind like that on my bottom . . . O well I suppose its because they were so plump and tempting in my short petticoat he couldnt resist".[53]

The relationship between the uses of women's clothing and women's preoccupation with and awareness of clothing, hardly needs arguing. Molly shows repeatedly that she has an eye and a memory for her wearing apparel and others', both women's and men's. Thus, in manuscript, she thinks concerning Boylan: "lovely stuff in that blue suit he had on and stylish tie and silk socks he's certainly well off".[54] In proof, this passage ends: "and socks with the skyblue silk things on them hes certainly welloff". After "welloff" Joyce adds "I know by the cut his clothes have and his heavy watch".[55]

Molly recalls her Spanish days:

> thats why I was afraid when that other ferocious old bull began to charge the banderilleros and the brutes of men shouting bravo toro sure the women were as bad ripping all the whole insides out of those poor horses

After "banderilleros" Joyce inserts "with the things in their hats". Then, after the newly introduced "the", he adds further "sashes and the 2". And after "bad" he inserts "in their nice white mantillas".[56]

Molly remembers the departure of a friend from Gibraltar: "she had a gorgeous wrap on her for the voyage". Following this phrase Joyce adds, in typescript: "made very peculiarly to one side like and it was extremely pretty".[57] In proof, after "wrap" he adds "of some special kind of blue colour".[58]

Molly is thinking about Mulvey: "my blouse open for his last day". After "day" Joyce adds "transparent kind of shirt he had I could see his chest pink".[59]

About the photograph of herself which Bloom showed to Stephen, Molly thinks: "its not good of me still I look young in it". After "me" Joyce inserts "I ought to have got it taken in drapery that never looks out of fashion".[60]

True to life, Molly has thoughts which we associate particularly with the feminine mind. She recalls "that old faggot Mrs Riordan": "I suppose she was pious because no man would look at her twice". After "twice" Joyce adds "I hope Ill never be like her".[61]

A little later Molly thinks: "I wish some or other would take me sometimes when he's there and kiss me in his arms". Apparently the printer has been guilty of an omission, as the typescript reads "some man".[62] In proof, Joyce changes "some" to "somebody", which he then replaces with the original "some man" [63]—eliminating the neutral "-body" so that Molly, as a female mind, again thinks of the somebody in terms of masculinity.

The maternal instinct in Molly also expresses itself: "supposing I risked having another not of him [Boylan] though still if he was married Im sure hed have a fine strong child but I dont know Poldy has more spunk in him". After the second "him" Joyce adds "yes thatd be awfully jolly".[64]

Molly's experience as a mother inspires an addition. She thinks: "an hour he was at them [her breasts] Im sure by the clock all the pleasure those men get out of a woman". After "clock" Joyce adds "like some kind of a big infant I had at me they want everything in their mouth".[65]

Molly considers the time: "a quarter after what an unearthly hour". After "hour" Joyce adds "I suppose theyre just getting up in China now combing their pigtails for the day".[66] At a later stage, after "combing" Joyce adds "out" [67]—completing a thought most likely to occur to a woman with thick long hair which she probably has to comb out each morning. It should also be remembered that we are dealing with the year 1904, when all women wore their hair long.

The possible return of Stephen Dedalus moves Molly to think: "first I want to do the place up someway". Joyce brings out the housewife in Molly by inserting, after this phrase, "the dust grows in it I think while Im asleep".[68]

Both cause and effect of Molly's particular experience as a woman is her perspicacity in all matters relating to sex. She is probably not exaggerating greatly when, in considering Dublin women, she thinks: "passion God help their poor head I knew more about men and life when I was 15 than theyll all know at 50".[69]

She recalls a choir party at which Leopold sprained his foot: "Miss Stack bringing him flowers the worst old ones she could find at the bottom of the basket". After "basket" Joyce adds, in proof: "with her old maids voice trying to imagine he was dying on account of her to never see thy

face again".[70] And between a later proof [71] and the published text, again after "basket", Joyce must have introduced "anything at all to get into a mans bedroom".

Regarding a former confessor Molly thinks: "he had a
nice fat hand the palm moist always I wouldn't mind
feeling it". After "it" Joyce inserts "neither would he Id
say by his bullneck".[72]

Of her experience with Boylan she thinks, in manuscript: "no I never in all my life felt anyone had one the
size of that to make you feel full up". Before "no" Joyce
inserts "he must have eaten oysters I think a few dozen".[73]
In proof, after "up" Joyce adds "he must have a whole
sheep after".[74]

In manuscript, Molly's observing eye has learned to
recognize vicarious affection: "she used to be always em-
bracing me Josie whenever he was there meaning him of
course". After "course" Joyce adds:

> glauming me over and when I said I washed up and
> down as far as possible asking me and did you wash
> possible the women are always egging on to that when he's
> there they know by his eye the kind he is what spoils him[75]

In proof, after "his" Joyce adds "sly"; after "eye", "blink-
ing a bit when they come out with something".[76] In a later
proof, after "bit" he adds "putting on the indifferent".[77]

Again in manuscript, Molly's wardrobe occupies her
attention: "Ive no clothes at all the men won't look at
you and women try to walk on you".[78] In proof, this passage has become: "I've no clothes at all cutting up this
old hat and patching up the other the men won't look at
you and women try to walk on you". After "on you" Joyce
adds "because they know youve no man then".[79]

Besides representing the eternal feminine, Molly lives
under and is conditioned by particular circumstances.

She gives evidence of the fact that she is the daughter of
a soldier: "I hate the mention of politics after the war
that Pretoria and Ladysmith and Bloemfontein where
Gardner, Lieut Stanley, G, 8th Bn, Somerset Lt. Infantry
killed". For "Somerset Lt. Infantry killed" Joyce sub-

stitutes "2nd East Lancs Rgt of enteric fever".[80] The historical detail [81] which Joyce introduces, not only gives us the feel of a mind of the time, but also prepares for a stroke of characterization. Almost immediately afterward, though in a later version, Molly thinks:

> they could have made their peace in the beginning or old oom Paul and the rest of the old Krugers go and fight it out between them instead of dragging on for years killing any finelooking men there were I love to see a regiment pass in review

After "were" Joyce adds "with their fever if he was even decently shot it wouldnt have been so mad".[82] The soldier's daughter might have condoned the loss of her man had he died in the field.[83]

Molly is proud of her military connection. She is thinking about Kathleen Kearney and her voice pupils:

> anything in the world to make themselves someway interesting theyd die down dead if ever they got a chance of walking down the Alameda on an officer's arm like me on the bandnight

After "interesting" Joyce adds "soldiers daughter am I ay and whose are you bootmakers and publicans I beg your pardon coach I thought you were a wheelbarrow".[84]

Molly's military background also influences her speech.[85] She remembers: "he [Bloom] was throwing his sheeps eyes at those two I tried to wink at him first". After "two" Joyce inserts "doing skirt duty up and down".[86]

Molly's upbringing in Gibraltar has left its mark, and the Spanish content of her mind is carefully built up. An addition to this influence is made in Bloom's memory of a night on which he went down to the pantry to get something for Molly: "What was it she wanted? The Malaga raisins. Before Rudy was born." After the second phrase Joyce inserts "Thinking of Spain" [87]—adding an insight beyond Bloom's mind into that of his wife.

The additions to this side of Molly in her own thought are understandably more numerous. In connection with a conciliatory mission to an employer of Bloom's, she re-

calls: "he gave me a great eye once or twice". For "eye"
Joyce substitutes "mirada".[88]

Molly considers the boredom of her existence: "who
did I get the last letter from O Mrs Dwenn now whatever
possessed her to write after so many years". Following
"years" Joyce inserts "to know the recipe I had for olla
podrida". Then, for the internationally known "olla
podrida" Joyce substitutes the indigenous "pisto madrileno" [89]—bringing us closer to native Spain.

Shortly afterward Molly thinks:

> he [Mulvey] wanted to touch mine with his for a moment
> but I wouldnt let him for fear you never know consumption
> or leave me with a child that old servant Ines told me that
> one drop even if it got into you at all

After "child" Joyce adds "embarazada".[90] One may suppose that Molly has recalled the key word in the old
servant's admonition, about which we then hear more.

Molly considers marital relations: "her husband found
it out well and if he did can he undo it". After "undo it"
Joyce inserts "hes coronado anyway whatever he does".[91]

Bloom's kiss revolts Molly: "pfooh the dirty brutes the
mere thought is enough of course a woman wants to be
embraced 20 times a day almost to make her look young".
After "enough" Joyce adds "I kiss the feet of you senorita
theres some sense in that didnt he kiss our halldoor yes
he did what a madman nobody understands his cracked
ideas but me still".[92]

Toward the close of her reverie Molly thinks of "the
Greeks and the jews and those handsome Moors all in
white like kings and the figtrees in the Alameda gardens".
After "jews" Joyce adds:

> and the fowl market all clucking and the poor donkeys
> slipping half asleep and the vague fellows in the cloaks
> asleep in the shade on the steps and the big wheels of the
> carts of the bulls

After "kings", he adds:

> asking you to sit down in their bit of a shop and Ronda
> with the old windows two glancing eyes a lattice hid and O

that awful deepdown torrent O and the sea the sea
crimson sometimes like fire and the glorious sunsets [93]

In a later galley, after "windows" Joyce inserts "of the
posadas"; after "hid", "for her lover to kiss the iron and
the night we stayed the watchman going about serene with
his lamp".[94] The straightforward Spanish additions are
obvious enough. But, as Gilbert has pointed out, Joyce
also has Molly's Spanish background exert an influence
upon her English, for "vague" and "serene" are "echoes
of common Spanish words she used to hear at Gibraltar;
vago, a vagrant, and *sereno*, the night-watchman's cry as
he goes his rounds, 'All's well—*sereno!*' " [95]

Another important aspect of Molly is her limited intellectual equipment. Her ignorance transpires chiefly in
her beliefs and in her language. Again and again her mind
throws out popular superstitions. She recalls the death of
Gardner, to whom she had given a ring which had been
presented to her "for luck" by Mulvey: "but they [the
Boers] were well beaten all the same as if it brought its
bad luck with it still it must have been pure 16 carrot gold
because it was very heavy". After "with it" Joyce adds
"like an opal or pearl".[96]

On the chamber pot Molly thinks: "easy O Lord how
noisy". Following this phrase Joyce adds "I hope theyre
bubbles on it for a wad of money from some fellow".[97]

A number of additions reveal Molly's faith in cards.
With regard to Stephen Dedalus she suddenly remembers:

> wait by God yes wait yes he was on the cards this morning
> when I laid out the deck a young stranger you met before I
> thought it meant him but hes no chicken nor a stranger
> either didnt I dream something too yes there was some-
> thing about poetry in it

After "deck" Joyce points up Molly's hope by inserting
"union with". After the first "stranger" he adds "neither
dark nor fair"; after "either":

> besides my face was turned the other way what was the 7th
> after that the 10 of spades for a journey by land then
> there was a letter on its way and scandals too the 3 queens

and the 8 of diamonds for a rise in society yes wait it all came out and 2 red 8s for new garments look at that and [98]

Molly is still thinking of Stephen: "if I can only get in with a handsome young poet at my age". After "age" Joyce inserts "Ill throw them the 1st thing in the morning till I see if the wishcard comes out or Ill try pairing the lady herself and see if he comes out".[99]

Concerning her husband Molly thinks: "so well he may sleep and sigh the great suggester and Im to be slooching around down in the kitchen to get his lordship his breakfast". After "suggester" Joyce adds "if he knew how he came out on the cards a dark man in some perplexity between 2 7s too in prison for Lord knows what he does that I don't know".[100]

The superstitiousness of what religion has adhered to Molly, is exemplified by her comment on an act of faith, part of an addition in typescript: "the candle I lit that evening in Whitefriars' street chapel for the month of May see it brought its luck".[101] Immediately before this thought, in proof, Molly recalls the thunderclap which had disturbed her sleep earlier: "till that thunder woke me up as if the world was coming to an end God be merciful to us I thought the heavens were coming down about us when I blessed myself and said a Hail Mary". After "about us" Joyce inserts "to punish us".[102] Forgetting the natural attitude which she usually maintains toward sex, Molly, in the moment of fear, tries to appease the wrathful thundergod.

Later, she considers:

atheists or whatever they call themselves go and wash the cobbles off themselves first then they go howling for the priest and they dying and why why because theyre afraid

After "afraid" Joyce adds "of hell on account of their bad conscience".[103]

As I have said, Molly's language, also, betrays her ignorance. To begin with, it abounds in error. While Joyce corrected the grammar of her Italian prototype, he brought Molly closer to her model by introducing mistakes.

When Molly remembers, "that thunder woke me up as if the world were coming to an end", Joyce changes "were" to "was".[104]

Molly recalls Bloom's behavior when she once denied a desire of his: "he slept on the floor half the night naked and wouldnt eat any breakfast or speak a word". After "naked" Joyce introduces a confusion of tenses difficult to match even in Molly's speech: "the way the jews used when somebody dies belonged to them".[105]

The memory of Boylan's behavior, in a passage part of which I have already cited, vexes Molly: "no that's no way for him has he no manners nor no refinement in his nature". Joyce adds one barbarism to another by inserting, after "nor no refinement", "nor nothing".[106] Later, he 'completes' the negation by inserting "no" between "nor" and "nothing".[107]

Molly's limited command of the idiom helps explain her difficulty with "Unusual polysyllables of foreign origin".[108] In manuscript Joyce adds the thought, concerning letters of condolence, "your sad bereavement symphathy I always make that mistake and newphew with you in".[109] A line runs through the first "h" in "symphathy" and another through the first "w" in "newphew". The author, however, did not indicate his intention clearly enough, for in proof the addition reads: "your sad bereavement sympathy I always make that mistake and nephew with you in". For the "p" in "sympathy" Joyce therefore substitutes "ph" with a line through the "h", writing beside it the instruction "(reproduisez ainsi)". Then, for the first "e" in "nephew" he substitutes "ew" with a line through the "w", repreating his instruction and at the same time changing "you" to "2 double yous"—a more likely error.[110] In other words, he has restored visual images as they run through Molly's mind, and, through them, the process of her corrections.[111]

Soon afterward, again in manuscript, while Molly considers a correspondence with Boylan, Joyce adds a thought in part of which she gropes for a polysyllable:

I could write the answer in bed to let him imagine me
short just a few words not those long crossed letters
Floey Dillon used to write to the fellow that jilted her out
of the ladies' letterwriter acting with precipat precip itancy
with equal candour the greatest earthly happiness answer
to a gentleman's proposal affirmatively [112]

In proof, besides a few irrelevant changes, the groping
phrase has become "precipit precipitancy". After "letterwriter" Joyce adds "when I told her to say a few simple
words he could twist how he liked not".[113] Molly would
convert her linguistic weakness into lovers' strategy.

From Gibraltar days she recalls Mrs. Rubio, who
domineered over her "because I didnt run into mass often
enough in Santa Maria to please her with all her miracles
of the saints and the sun dancing 3 times on Easter
Sunday morning". After "morning" Joyce adds "and when
the priest was going by with the *vatican* to the dying
blessing herself for his Majestad".[114]

Joyce gives Molly an awareness of her intellectual limita-
tions when she thinks about her daughter: "such an idea
for him to send the girl down there to learn to take photographs only hed do a thing like that". After "photographs"
Joyce adds "on account of his grandfather instead of sending her to Skerry's academy where shed have to learn not
like me".[115] Later, after "me" he inserts "getting all ls at
school".[116]

No wonder, then, that Molly's general level of speech
lies among the lower reaches of English usage. To heighten
this effect Joyce puts into her mouth a considerable number of colloquialisms. One addition, the final form of
which I have already cited, shows Joyce at work col-
loquializing Molly's expression: "yes thatd be awfully
jolly" began as "yes that would be awfully jolly".[117]

Impatient of possible exposure during her projected
trip to Belfast with Boylan, Molly exclaims: "O let them
all go and smother themselves for all I care". Joyce replaces the second "all" with "the fat lot".[118]

The coming on of menstruation gives Molly something
further to exclaim about: "O let me up out of this pooh".
After "O" Joyce inserts "Jamesy".[119]

Molly considers: "I think Ill cut all this hair off me there scalding me I might look like a young girl". After "girl" Joyce adds "wouldnt he get the takein the next time he turned up my clothes Id give anything to watch his face". Then Joyce replaces "takein" with "great suckin", and after "clothes" he adds "on me".[120]

But Joyce does not rest content with a highly colloquial idiom for Molly. As a Dubliner who has not been much standardized by education, she would also be likely to show the influence of dialect upon her speech. Therefore, Joyce gives her a good proportion of dialect usage.

Thus, when Molly thinks concerning Bloom, "of course he prefers hanging about the house", Joyce changes "hanging" to "plottering".[121]

In a context one version of which I treated earlier, Molly thinks: "Kathleen Kearney and her lot of squealers they'd die down dead if they ever got a chance of walking down the Alameda on an officer's arm like me on the bandnight". After "squealers" Joyce adds "*skitting* around talking about politics they know as much about as my backside anything in the world to make themselves someway interesting".[122]

On the chamber pot Molly thinks: "I remember one time I could do it out straight whistling like a man almost". Joyce replaces "do" with "scout".[123]

Concerning a gynecologist Molly remembers: "still I liked him when he sat down to write the thing out frowning so severe his nose intelligent like that you be damned you lying bitch". For "bitch" Joyce substitutes "strap".[124]

Molly returns to the subject of her latest adultery: "Ill let him [Bloom] know if thats what he wanted that his wife is fucked and damn well fucked too not by him 5 or 6 times running". For "running" Joyce substitutes "handrunning".[125]

Another important aspect of Molly, in which she contrasts with her mild husband, is her irritability. Her frustration as Mrs. Bloom, her husband's ordering of breakfast, and the inception of menstruation less than four days before Boylan is next to arrive, add fuel to a temperamental petulance. Her speech, as a result, is full of twitching impatiences, a number of which Joyce introduces in revision.

Suspecting that Bloom has spent the evening with another woman, Molly recalls his flirtation with a servant: "I couldn't even touch him if I thought he was with a dirty liar and sloven like that one". After "dirty" Joyce adds "barefaced".[126]

About the trip to Belfast Molly thinks: "O I suppose there'll be the usual idiots of men gaping at us". Following "us", in manuscript, Joyce adds "with their eyes as stupid as ever they can be".[127] In proof, after "can" he inserts "possibly".[128]

Molly considers Bloom's late return: "well thats a nice hour for him to be coming home at to anybody". After "hour" Joyce charges Molly's grievance more highly by inserting "of the night".[129]

In one passage, Joyce makes alterations which seem to be intended to render a changing attitude. Molly recalls the boredom of Gibraltar: "as bad as now with the hands hanging off me looking out of the window if there was a nice fellow even in the opposite house the meat and the coalmans bell". After "house" Joyce adds:

> that idiot medical in Holles street the nurse was after when I put on my gloves and hat at the window to show I was going out not a notion what I meant arent they thick youd want to put it up on a big poster for them not even if you shake their hands twice where does their great intelligence come in Id like to know

Then, as if realizing that Molly's first thought of a man she had desired would be likely to be favorable, Joyce deletes "idiot". And after "twice" he adds "he didnt recognize me either outside Westland row chapel".[130] As Molly dwells on the subject, she becomes exasperated. In a later galley, Joyce introduces more scorn with more signs: after "thick" he adds "never understand what you say even"; he deletes "their" before "hands", and after "twice" adds "with the left"; after "either" he adds "when I half frowned at him"; and after "know", the final fling:

"grey matter they have it all in their tail if you ask me".[131]

From such general irritability it is only a step to temper. In revising, Joyce heightens Molly's inflammability. She considers a pair of stockings that are laddered after one day's wear: "I could have brought them back to Sparrows this morning and made them change them only not to run the risk of walking into him and ruining the whole thing". For "made them" Joyce substitutes "kick up a row and make that one", and after "not to" he adds "upset myself and".[132]

In private Molly does not curb her temper. She remembers her daughter's refusal to go on an errand: "till I gave her a damn fine crack across the ear for herself she had me that exasperated that was the last time she turned on the teartrap". In manuscript, after "herself" Joyce adds "take that for answering me like that".[133] In proof, to heighten Molly's anger, he alters "a" to "2" and "crack" to "cracks". After "like that" he adds "and that for your impudence"; after "exasperated", "of course because she has nobody to command her as she said herself well if he doesn't correct her faith I will".[134] In a later galley, after "course" he inserts an explanation for Molly's violence: "I was badtempered too because how was it I didnt sleep the night before cheese I ate was it and I told her over and over again not to leave knives crossed like that".[135] In a still later galley, further extenuation is added: between "course" and "I" Joyce inserts "contradicting", and after "how was it" he adds "there was a weed in the tea or".[136] But, explaining or no explaining, Molly is easily angered.

Occasionally, her temper goads her to cruelty. She recalls a boatride on which Bloom proved a wretched oarsman: "in his flannel trousers Id like to have tattered them down off him before all the people and give him what that one calls flagellate do him all the good in the world". Molly may not be at home with the 'jawbreaker,' but Joyce makes certain that she finds the action it represents congenial: after "flagellate" he adds "till he was black and blue".[137]

Incensed at the thought of her husband's unsatisfying

attentions, Molly threatens: "I'll make him do it again if he doesn't mind himself I wonder was it her Josie". After "himself" Joyce adds "and sleep down in the coalcellar".[138] Later, after "coalcellar" he adds "with the blackbeetles".[139] Still later, he deletes "down" after "sleep" to introduce a further refinement before "sleep": "lock him down to".[140]

In addition to temper, Molly reveals a streak of spitefulness. About her affair with Bartell d'Arcy, she thinks: "Ill tell him [Bloom] about that some day not now and surprise him he thinks nothing can happen without him knowing". After "surprise him" Joyce adds "ay and Ill take him there and show the very place too".[141] Later, between "too" and "he" Joyce inserts "so now there you are".[142] Still later, between "are" and "he" Joyce adds "like it or lump it".[143]

Molly makes plans for the concert: "yes by God Ill get that big fan mended". After "mended" Joyce adds "make them ["Kathleen Kearney and her lot of squealers"] burst with envy".[144]

In an insertion already cited, Molly explains this whole side of her character by a generalization: "I suppose its all the troubles we have makes us so snappy".[145]

One of the most important of Molly's "troubles" I have reserved for lengthier treatment. Throughout her reverie runs the motif of fretting poverty. Directly and indirectly she reveals the restrictions which her husband's improvidence has placed upon her. She remembers: "when I was in the DBC with Poldy laughing and trying to listen I was waggling my foot". After "foot" Joyce adds "we both ordered 2 teas and plain bread and butter".[146] Somewhat later, she reverts to the subject: "always hanging out of them for money in a restaurant we have to be thankful for our cup of tea even". In manuscript, after "even" Joyce adds "to be noticed".[147] In typescript, the passage concludes "for our cup of tea as a great compliment to be noticed", and before "cup" Joyce inserts "mangy".[148] In proof, after "restaurant" Joyce adds "for the bit you put down your throat"; after "tea", the belittling Anglo-Irish "itself".[149]

Molly, in manuscript, considers her wardrobe:

and the four paltry handkerchiefs about 6/– in all sure you can't get on in this world without clothes the men won't look at you and women try to walk on you for the four years more I have of life up to 35

Joyce replaces "clothes" with "style I've no clothes at all".[150] In proof, the passage has become:

and the four paltry handkerchiefs about 6/– in all sure you can't get on in this world without style all going in food and rent when I get it I'll lash it around if I buy a pair of old brogues itself do you like new those new shoes yes how much were they I've no clothes at all cutting up an old hat and patching up the other the men won't look at you and women try to walk on you for the four years more I have of life up to 35

After "around" Joyce adds "I tell you in fine style I always want to throw a handful of tea into the pot measuring and mincing".[151] In a later galley, after "at all" he adds "the brown costume and the skirt and jacket and the one at the cleaners 3 whats that for any woman".[152] Still later, he makes Molly poverty-conscious for a further reason: after "on you" in a third galley he adds "because they know youve no man then",[153] and after "then" in a fourth he inserts "with all the things getting dearer every day".[154]

When Molly thinks, "I havent even a decent nightdress", Joyce emphasizes her irritation by changing "a" to "one".[155]

Molly feels "some wind in me better go easy not wake him have him at it again slobbering after washing every bit of myself back belly and sides". Following "sides" Joyce adds "if we had even a bath itself".[156]

About menstruation Molly thinks: "isnt it simply sickening that night it came on me like that the one time we were in a box that Michael Gunn gave him". Joyce again emphasizes Molly's awareness by adding, after "one", "and only".[157]

Looking back upon her married life, Molly observes: "God here we are as bad as ever after sixteen years every time were just getting on right something happens". After "years" Joyce points up the chronic poverty of the Blooms by adding "how many houses were we in at all".[158] At a later stage, after "all", he inserts a travelogue of impecuniosity:

> Raymond terrace and Ontario terrace and Lombard street and Holles street and he goes about whistling every time were on the run again his huguenots or the frogs march and then the City Arms hotel worse and worse says Warden Daly that charming place on the landing always somebody inside praying then leaving all their stinks after them always know who was in there last

Then Joyce completes the account by adding, after the newly introduced "march", "pretending to help the men with our 4 sticks of furniture".[159]

Offsetting Molly's personal and economic frustration is her inveterate buoyancy, which is abetted by her talent for singing. In revising, Joyce builds up our awareness of this aspect of Molly by introducing musical associations.[160]

Molly remembers: "when I threw the penny to that lame sailor". In typescript, after "sailor" Joyce adds "for England home and beauty".[161] In proof, this musical association begets another: after "beauty" Joyce adds, appropriately, "when I was whistling there is a charming girl I love".[162]

Molly told her first lover that she was engaged "to the son of a Spanish nobleman and he believed that I was to be married to him in three years time there's many a true word spoken in jest". In typescript, after "nobleman" Joyce adds "named Don Miguel de la Flora", and after "jest" "the flowers that bloom in the spring trala".[163] But in proof he replaces the snatch with "there is a flower that bloometh"[164]—a happier association, since in the course of her reverie Molly recalls two other airs by the same composer, one from the same work as the air here added.[165]

Thoughts on poetry evoke a song:

> where softly sighs of love the light guitar where poetry is in the air the blue sea and the moon shining so beautifully coming back on the nightboat from Tarifa the guitar

that fellow played was so expressive will ever go back there again all new faces two glancing eyes a lattice hid I'll sing that for him [Stephen] they're my eyes if he's anything of a poet two eyes as softly bright as love's young star aren't those beautiful words as love's young star

Joyce alters the second "softly" to "darkly" [166] and, in a later galley, the first "young" to "own".[167] The reasons for these changes are implicit in the words of the song, *In Old Madrid*, which begins: "Long years ago in old Madrid, Where softly sighs of love the light guitar, Two sparkling eyes, a lattice hid, Two eyes as darkly bright as love's own star!" [168] In the earlier galley, Joyce corrects the second of three inaccuracies,[169] a confusion the source of which lies before us; in the later galley, by correcting the first specimen of the third inaccuracy, he causes Molly's mind to *move* into error.

Bloom crowds the bed, and Molly, irritated, breaks out: "O move over your big carcass out of that for the love of Mike so well he may sleep". After "Mike" Joyce adds "listen to him the winds that waft my sighs to thee".[170]

Memories of Gibraltar again evoke *In Old Madrid*. Molly recalls "those handsome Moors all in white like kings and the figtrees in the Alameda gardens". Part of an insertion after "kings", as I have shown in another connection, is "two glancing eyes a lattice hid".[171]

Besides presenting Molly, the long monologue with which *Ulysses* closes serves another and multiple characterizing purpose. Through Molly's eyes we gain new information and, more importantly, a new 'slant,' that of a woman, on many of her fellow characters. Chief among these, understandably, is her husband. As her reverie unfolds, we see again, but this time through the eyes of his faithless, disparaging, yet withal devoted wife, many of the traits of Bloom which I have discussed elsewhere.[172] Concerning the monologue Joyce wrote to Budgen, then in the British consular service, "It is the indispensable countersign to Bloom's passport to eternity." [173]

In revising, Joyce augments the number of points at which Molly's thought meets our memory of the Bloom we have come to know during the preceding seventeen hours. In the penultimate episode, between a list of instances of Molly's "deficient mental development" and a succeeding question as to how Bloom had attempted to remedy her ignorance, Joyce makes a preparatory interpolation:

> What compensated in the false balance of her intelligence for these and such deficiencies of judgment regarding persons, places and things?
> The false apparent parallelism of all perpendicular arms of all balances, true by construction. The counterbalance of proficiency of judgment regarding one person, proved true by experiment.[174]

Who the person may be, it is superfluous to ask. In the final episode, the interpolation is borne out.

The thrifty temperance which Bloom practiced during the day is echoed in additions. Molly thinks: "he has sense enough not to squander every penny piece he earns down their gullets goodfornothings". After "gullets" Joyce inserts "and looks after his wife and family".[175]

Bloom's curiosity inspires additions. Molly considers

> a picnic suppose we all gave 5/ each and or let him pay it and invite some other woman for him who Mrs Fleming and drove out to the furry glen or the strawberry beds with some cold veal and ham mixed sandwiches

After "beds" Joyce adds "wed have him examining all the horses toenails first no not with Boylan there yes". Then, after "first" he adds further "like he does with the letters".[176]

One of Molly's memories of Bloom's courtship reminds us, in an insertion already cited, of his didactic streak: "explaining and rigmaroling about religion and persecution he wont let you enjoy anything naturally".[177] Another gibe at this trait of Bloom's is introduced somewhat later. Molly has just expressed her discomfort at Bloom's crowding of the bed: "so well he may sleep and Im to be slooching around down in the kitchen to get his lordship his breakfast". After "sleep" Joyce adds "and sigh the great suggester".[178]

The humanitarian in Bloom wins Molly's affection. In manuscript, Joyce adds the thought "still I like that in him polite to old women like that".[179] In typescript, after the second "that" he inserts "and waiters".[180] In proof, after "waiters" he introduces "and beggars too but not always".[181] In a later proof, after "too" he adds "hes not proud out of nothing".[182]

Bloom's mild, unpugnacious disposition, so strongly contrasted with his wife's, comes out in Molly's memory of a conjugal row: "he began it not me when he said about Our Lord being a carpenter and the first socialist still he knows a lot of mixed up things". After "socialist" Joyce adds "he annoyed so much I couldnt put him into a temper".[183]

Bloom's considerateness, now directed toward Molly, elicits her gratitude. She thinks:

> anyhow I hope hes not going to get in with those medicals leading him astray to imagine hes young again coming in waking me up at 2 in the morning it must be if not more what do they find to gabber about all night

As if realizing that it would be unlike Bloom to disturb anyone, Joyce deletes "waking me up", and following "more" adds "still he had the manners not to wake me".[184]

After Molly thinks that, if Bloom should fall seriously ill, it would be better for him to go to a hospital, she observes: "but I suppose I'd have to dring it into him for a month". Following "month" Joyce introduces the philanderer in Bloom: "yes and then wed have a hospital nurse next thing on the carpet or a nun maybe like the photo he has shes as much as Im not". Then after "carpet" Joyce adds further "have him staying there till they throw him out"; before "photo", "smutty".[185]

Like the narrator of the *Cyclops* episode, whose words she echoes,[186] Molly considers Bloom a cotquean: "of course he prefers plottering about the house so you cant stir with him any side what's your programme today". After "today" Joyce adds "I wish hed even smoke a pipe like father to get the smell of a man".[187]

Bloom is not man enough for Molly, not only on the marriage couch and about the house, but also in business. Thus far, in the changes we have watched Joyce make, Molly has only corroborated traits in her husband which we already know. But she also gives us a new view of the "great Suggester" as a chronic bungler. Shortly after the thought "I hate an unlucky man" Molly considers that Boylan "must have been a bit late because it was ¼ after 3 when I saw the 2 Dedalus girls coming from school". After "school" Joyce adds "I never know the time even that watch he [Bloom] gave me never seems to go properly Id want to get it looked after".[188]

Molly lacks confidence in Bloom as an agent: "I told him get that [face lotion] made up in the same place and dont forget it God only knows whether he did Ill know by the bottle anyway". After "did" Joyce adds "after all I said to him".[189] Later, Joyce goes back to prepare for this change by inserting, after "told him", "over and over again".[190]

Again, through Molly's eyes we see the Bloom who is full of business schemes that never come off: "musical academy he was going to make like all the things he told father he was going to do and me but I saw through him". In manuscript, after "make" Joyce inserts "on the first floor drawingroom with a brassplate".[191] In proof, after "brassplate" he adds "or Blooms private hotel he suggested".[192] In a later proof, after "suggested" he adds further "go and ruin himself altogether the way his father did down in Ennis".[193]

Molly is considering the possibility of an affair with Stephen:

> itll be a change the Lord knows to have an intelligent person to talk to about yourself not always listening to him and Billy Prescotts ad and Keyess ad and Tom the Devils ad Im sure hes very distinguished

After the last "ad" Joyce inserts a generalization which Molly may claim is based upon experience: "then if anything goes wrong in their business we have to suffer".[194]

Joyce does not allow us to forget that no character knows Bloom as thoroughly as does his wife. She thinks: "when hes like that he cant keep a thing back". After "back" Joyce inserts "I know every turn in him".[195]

Molly, as I have said, gives us her view of other characters as well as of her husband. She recalls a former confessor:

> when I used to go to Father Corrigan he touched me father and what harm if he did where and I said on the canal bank like a fool but whereabouts on your person on the leg behind high up was it yes rather high up was it where you sit down yes O Lord couldnt he say bottom right out and have done with it what has that got to do with it and did you whatever way he put it I forget no father and I always think of the real father what did he want to know for when I already confessed it to God he had a nice fat hand the palm moist always I wouldn't mind feeling it neither would he Id say by his bullneck in his horsecollar

Then, as in the case of Father Conmee, Joyce introduces the priestly aura, by adding, after "person", "my child".[196] The thought of Lenehan evokes a memory:

> that sponger he was making free with me after the Glencree dinner coming back that long joult over the featherbed mountain I first noticed him at dessert when I was cracking the nuts with my teeth

After "mountain" Joyce inserts "after the lord Mayor looking at me with his dirty eyes Val Dillon".[197] And later, after "Dillon" he adds "that big heathen".[198]

Following Molly's thought of Dignam as a "comical little teetotum", Joyce inserts "always stuck up in some pub corner and her or her son waiting Bill Bailey won't you please come home what men".[199]

Yet, despite the importance of Molly's reverie to the totality of our conception of her fellow characters, "it is absurd," as one critic has written, "to take the . . . final chapter as a submission of the whole narrative to Molly's . . . stream of consciousness. We as readers do the sum-

ming up, surely, even if we do it with the aid of her necessary final information." [200]

ii

In improving upon his characters, Joyce evinces
a hundred-eyed alertness to the possibilities of fuller and
more immediate realization.

Upon Molly Bloom, his second great, and his concluding, creation in *Ulysses*, Joyce lavishes effort, successfully,
to produce a portrait of the eternal feminine. Her physique, her sexuality, her acceptance of the body, her am-
bivalent attitude toward the male, her technique of attraction, the femininity of her mind, her perceptiveness
in sexual matters—all these are steadily built up. Being,
besides Woman, a woman, Molly grows in the process of
revision as the daughter of a soldier; as one whose mind
is partly Spanish in content; whose intellectual equipment,
as her beliefs and her use of language indicate, is limited;
whose short temper, further abbreviated by poverty, is
offset by a buoyancy which is abetted by her talent for
singing; whose views on her fellow characters, her husband
in particular, serve to round out our conception of the
microcosm that was Dublin on June 16, 1904.

7 STYLISTIC REALISM IN ULYSSES

> In the longer work described in the opening section of the essay on Stephen Dedalus, the present essay is one of two chapters on style. The other chapter, on "Varieties of Style," will, I trust, offset any impression that Joyce's writing can be ticketed with a single label. (For a summary of the other chapter, see "The Language of James Joyce's Ulysses" in Langue et Littérature: Actes du VIIIᵉ Congrès de la Fédération Internationale des Langues et Littératures Modernes [Paris, 1961], pp. 306–7.)

IN ANY DISCUSSION of style which concerns Joyce, one would do well to bear in mind Stendhal's definition: "le style est ceci: *Ajouter à une pensée donnée toutes les circonstances propres à produire tout l'effet que doit produire cette pensée.*"[1]

Of primary importance in the achievement of style, it need hardly be said, is precision in the use of words. Joyce's reputation on this score has eclipsed even that of his master Flaubert. The process of revision demonstrates beyond peradventure the fundamental role which the *mot juste* plays in Joyce's extraordinarily faithful realism.

For example, in a manuscript notebook we are told that under the leaf of his hat Stephen Dedalus "watched through quivering peacock lashes the southing sun." Joyce moves from "quivering peacock" to "peacockquivering", then to "peacocktwinkling", and finally, achieving the published version, to "peacocktwittering".[2]

Miles Crawford, the newspaper editor, wishes to see his dayfather:

Where's what's his name?
  He looked about him round his loud unanswering ma-
  chines.
  —Monks, sir?
  —Ay. Where's Monks?

After "sir?" Joyce adds in galley proof, "a voice asked from
behind the castingbox." [3] The impression of unbodied
source made by the speech of an unseen speaker is exactly
reproduced.[4]

Later in the day, from "the window of the D. B. C.
Buck Mulligan gaily, and Haines gravely, gazed down on
the viceregal carriages". Joyce alters "carriages" to "equi-
page",[5] giving us, instead of undistinguished vehicles, a
carriage of state with all that accompanies it, in this case
horses, outriders, and the following carriage—the whole
scene.

When the citizen takes "out his handkerchief to swab
himself dry", we read:

> The muchtreasured and intricately embroidered ancient
> Irish facecloth attributed to Solomon of Droma and Manus
> Tomaltach, authors of the Book of Ballymote, was then
> carefully produced and called forth prolonged admiration.
> The scenes depicted on it are as wonderfully beautiful and
> the pigments as delicate as when the Sligo illuminators
> gave free rein to their artistic fantasy long long ago in the
> time of the Barmecides.

Among other changes, Joyce replaces the colorless "it"
with "the emunctory field".[6] With this impressively exact
phrase he punctures the passage even as he inflates it.

To enter his home, at the end of the day, Bloom
"raised the latch of the area door by the exertion of force
at its free arm". For "free arm" Joyce substitutes "freely
moving flange".[7]

As we all know, however, precision does not denote
only exactness with the independent word. There is also
precision within a context—appropriateness. In this kind,
too, Joyce excels.

At twilight,

A lost long candle wandered up the sky from Mirus bazaar in aid of funds for Mercer's hospital and broke, drooping, and shed a cluster of violet but one white stars.

Joyce alters "aid" to "search",[8] adapting a phrase from the placard advertising the bazaar[9] to one which, fitting into its context more appositely, gives the whole sentence a unity of effect it formerly did not possess, and at the same time accords with the anthropomorphic impressions which Bloom has, in his drowsy state, of other inanimate things mentioned in the same paragraph.

In another passage we may watch Joyce at work selecting the precisely appropriate word. To men's praises of Bloom, Joyce adds the following:

[*Women whisper eagerly.*]

> A MILLIONAIRESS
> [*richly*] Isn't he simply wonderful?
> A NOBLEWOMAN
> [*nobly*] All that man has seen!
> A FEMINIST
> [*masculinely*] And done![10]

The adverb qualifying the first speech did not come to Joyce at one stroke. He first wrote "entl" ("ent[husiastically]"? [the *t* is uncrossed; the presumed *h*, only half-completed]), then he deleted that and wrote "(adoringly)", and finally he deleted that for the highly appropriate "*richly*", which consists with the millionairess as "*nobly*" does with the noblewoman and "*masculinely*" with the feminist.

Among Bloom's memories of Milly as an infant, is "a doll, a boy, a sailor she threw away:". Joyce alters "threw" to "cast".[11] And how much more appropriate it is that the sailor should have been *cast away*.

When he can do so without violence to dramatic propriety, Joyce even manipulates the style of his characters in the interest of precision. The reader who deals with the final text cannot be aware of the improvement.

Even Bloom, who might well be forgiven a lack of precision, is not immune to such revision. In the morning he considers: "Dislike dressing together. Cut myself shaving." Joyce alters "Cut" to "Nicked".[12]

At the funeral Bloom recalls Dignam's appearance: "Blazing face: redhot. Cure for a red nose. Drink like the devil till it turns puce." For "puce" Joyce substitutes "adelite" [13]—and, since adelite is gray, while puce would still give us red (though a weak red), the cure is now complete.

Later in the same episode, we again see Joyce at work adding precision through the mind of Bloom. An interpolation begins as "Only a mother and child ever buried in the one coffin." Then, before "child" Joyce adds "newborn". Finally, he changes "newborn" to "deadborn",[14] achieving complete accuracy.

Bloom recalls a snatch from *The Young May Moon*: "Glowworm's lamp is gleaming, love." Changing "lamp" to "la-amp",[15] Joyce accounts exactly for the two notes to which the word is sung.[16]

But genius can err, and in a number of revisions Joyce confutes Stephen's proud claim to the contrary,[17] for these changes create difficulties, particularly with respect to precision.

Mr. Deasy, in paying Stephen Dedalus, lays two notes on the table. "—Two, he said, stowing his pocketbook away." In manuscript, Joyce inserts "strapping and" before "stowing" [18] without eliminating the awkwardness of "strapping . . . his pocketbook away."

Bloom has hurried downstairs to save the burning kidney: "By prodding a prong of the fork under the kidney he detached it and turned it over on its back." For "over" Joyce substitutes "turtle" [19]—in itself certainly an improvement, except that it introduces a tautology which Joyce does not eliminate.

In the passage describing Bloom's exit from All Hallows Church, the following sentence is added: "He stood a moment unseeing by the cold stone stoup while before him and behind two worshippers dipped furtive hands in the low tide of holy water." [20] Later "cold stone stoup" becomes "cold black marble bowl", [21] which, while it adds precision in further qualifying the basin, eliminates the specific ecclesiastical "stoup" for the general "bowl".

Lenehan has just told M'Coy how Tom Rochford once saved a man's life:

—The act of a hero, he [Lenehan] said.
At the Dolphin he halted.
—This way, he said, walking to the right. I want to pop into Lynam's to see Sceptre's starting price. What's the time by your gold watch and chain?

Joyce changes the second sentence to read: "At the Dolphin they halted to allow the ambulance car to gallop past them." [22] He fails, however, to make the now necessary revision, in the third sentence, of "he said" to "Lenehan said". As it stands, the statement leaves the reader uncertain who the speaker is, and the doubt is resolved only later, when M'Coy replies.

In the penultimate episode, a confusion is introduced as another difficulty is eliminated.

What marks of special hospitality did the host [Bloom] show his guest [Stephen]?
Relinquishing his right to the moustache cup of imitation crown Derby presented to him by his only daughter, Millicent, he drank from a cup identical with that of his guest and served to his guest and, in reduced measure, to himself, the cream usually reserved for the breakfast of his wife Marion (Molly).

Were there marks of hospitality which he contemplated but suppressed, reserving them for another and for himself on future occasions?
The reparation of a fissure of the length of 1½ inches in the right side of his guest's jacket. A gift to his guest of one of the four lady's handkerchiefs, if and when ascertained to be in a presentable condition.

Was the guest conscious of and did he acknowledge these marks of hospitality?
His attention was directed to them by his host jocosely and he accepted them seriously as they drank in silence.

The third answer, in this version, implies that the guest could *accept* marks of hospitality which the host contemplated but suppressed. Joyce therefore transposes the last two units of question and answer,[23] so that the acceptance now relates to marks of hospitality actually shown.

The revision, however, introduces a confusion of reference. In the old version, it was perfectly clear that Bloom was "he" who "contemplated but suppressed", for the subject of the preceding answer—"he"—, as well as the seven other pronominal forms in the statement, referred to "the host" of the first question. But in the new version, both subjects of the preceding sentence—"His attention" and "he"—refer to "the guest". To clear up this detail required only the substitution of "the host" for "he" before "contemplated"—an improvement which Joyce failed to make here and did not fail to make in neighboring passages.[24]

Through a mirror Bloom sees the "optical reflection of several inverted volumes with scintillating titles on the two bookshelves opposite." After "volumes" Joyce adds "improperly arranged and not in the order of their common letters".[25] As a result, "with scintillating titles" is awkwardly distant from "volumes" and uncomfortably close to "letters".

But these few lapses should not blind us to the fact that the great mass of Joyce's innumerable revisions represent improvement of one kind or another. And now I pass to another kind, namely, specification. A writer who strives for precision will probably also aim at being concrete and specific. In a whole group of changes Joyce moves steadily from the general to the particular.

Near the opening of the first episode, Stephen, leaning on the parapet of the Martello tower, "looked down on the water." From a preceding sentence we know that "the water" is "Dublin bay",[26] but it is unqualified; we know nothing more about it than that it is the water of Dublin Bay. Joyce deletes the period to add "and on the mailboat clearing the harbour mouth of Kingstown." [27]—and at once the bay has assumed the detailed features of a particular scene. The further specification by kind of boat and by place-name needs no comment. But the location of the boat introduces perspective. Stephen's general view, starting with the whole undifferentiated expanse of the harbor, converges upon a particular point, the mouth; and his awareness of the mouth implies awareness of the shores running round to it, and of the sea beyond. More important still, with the boat in the act of leaving the harbor, the hitherto inert scene has taken on motion. Again and again, as we shall see,[28] Joyce introduces movement.

And the mailboat goes on moving. Toward the close of the episode, Haines "gazed over the bay, empty save for a sail tacking by the Muglins." After "for" Joyce adds "the smokeplume of the mailboat vague on the bright skyline and".[29] The ship has sailed, in the course of the episode, from the harbor mouth to a point near the horizon on the open sea.

When the Citizen threw the tinbox at Bloom, the "observatory at Dunsink registered in all eleven shocks and there is no record extant of a similar seismic disturbance in our island since the earthquake of 1534, the year of the rebellion of Silken Thomas." After "shocks" Joyce adds technical specifications: ", all of the fifth grade of Mercalli's scale,".[30]

At midnight, in answer to a stern summons from the watch, Bloom, "(*Scared, makes Masonic signs.*)".[31] Between this galley and publication, for the indefinite last three words Joyce substitutes specific signs: "*hats himself, steps back then, plucking at his heart and lifting his right forearm on the square, he gives the sign and dueguard of fellowcraft*".

Bloom is about to have his babies:

A NURSETENDER

Embrace me tight, dear. You'll be soon over it. Tight, dear.

Joyce changes the anonymous "A NURSETENDER" to "*Mrs Thornton*", whom we have already met.[32]

Almost immediately afterward, Bloom hints that he may be a messiah:

A LAYBROTHER

Then perform a miracle.

Joyce changes "A LAYBROTHER" to "BROTHER BUZZ",[33] whom, also, we have met before.[34]

Soon afterward, again, a general occupational term is replaced by the name of a specific practitioner already known to us:

A BUSHRANGER

What did you do in the cattlecreep behind Kilbarrack?

For "A BUSHRANGER" Joyce substitutes "*Crab*".[35]

Later in the same episode, "(*The widow woman, her snubnose and cheeks flushed with deathtalk, fears and Tunny's tawny sherry, hurries by in her weeds, her bonnet awry.*" For "*The*" Joyce substitutes "Mrs Dignam," [36] whose husband's funeral Bloom had attended in the morning.

When Bloom and Stephen had their cocoa, we learn, Bloom drank his more quickly, "having the advantage of ten seconds at the initiation and taking three sips to his opponent's one." Joyce deletes the period and adds, "six to two, nine to three." [37] By this addition the figures first given are transformed from an abstract mathematical ratio into part of a specific relative progression by the drinkers, one of whom, it now appears, emptied his cup in nine sips, the other in three.[38]

Bloom and Stephen construct scenes suggested by the former's unrealized project of an advertising showcart.[39] Then Stephen narrates his *Pisgah Sight of Palestine* or *Parable of the Plums*, which,

> with the preceding scene [Stephen's construction] and with others unnarrated but existent by implication, to which add essays on various subjects composed during schoolyears, seemed to him [Bloom] to contain in itself and in conjunction with the personal equation certain possibilities of financial, social, personal and sexual success, [40]

After "subjects" Joyce adds "or moral apothegms (e.g., *My Favourite Hero* or *Procrastination is the Thief of Time*)".[41]

As for precision, so for specification, Joyce unobtrusively

manages the thought of his characters. Thus, Bloom, thinking about the railway lost property office, generalizes:

> Astonishing the things people leave behind them in trains and cloak rooms. What do they be thinking about? Women too. Incredible. There's a little watch up there on the roof of the bank to test those glasses by.

After "Incredible." Joyce adds a pair of specific examples: "Last year travelling to Ennis had to pick up that farmer's daughter's bag and hand it to her at Limerick junction. Unclaimed money too." [42]

Bloom is thinking about menstruation: "All kinds of crazy longings. Girl in Tranquilla convent that nun told me liked to smell rock oil." Between the generalization and the specimen Joyce inserts another specimen: ".Licking pennies." [43]

Bloom's thoughts are again on women:

> Poor idiot! His wife has her work cut out for her. Sharp as needles they are. When I said to Molly the man at the corner of Cuffe street was goodlooking, thought she might like, twigged at once he had a false arm. Had too. Where they get that? Handed down from father to mother to daughter, I mean.

The rest of the paragraph contains further specimens of feminine sharpness. But let us confine ourselves to the changes in the passage cited. Here Joyce works Bloom's thought up to the generalization on sharpness by introducing specific examples before it: ".Never see them sit on a bench marked *Wet Paint*. Eyes all over them. Look under the bed for what's not there." [44] In a later galley, after "that?", Joyce adds still another specimen: ". Typist going up Roger Greene's stairs two at a time to show her understandings." [45]

Molly looks back upon her courtship:

> then [Leopold] writing a letter every morning sometimes twice a day I liked the way he made love then he knew the way to take a woman then I wrote the night he kissed my heart at Dolphin's barn I couldn't describe it simply it makes you feel like nothing on earth

After "woman" Joyce introduces another specimen of Bloom's knowledge: "when he sent me the 8 big poppies because mine was the 8th".[46]

Molly recalls her last day with Mulvey: "I was a bit wild after coming back". Following "after" Joyce introduces a specimen of Molly's wildness: "when I blew out the old bag the biscuits were in from Albertis and exploded it Lord what a bang all the woodcocks and pigeons screaming".[47] Another specimen, already embedded in the text, follows shortly after.[48]

Molly plans to buy fish for the day which has just begun: "anyway Im sick of that everlasting butchers meat or [it occurs to her] a picnic". After "butchers meat" Joyce begins to specify by inserting "from Buckleys".[49] Later, after "Buckleys" he adds specimens of the meat: "loin chops and leg beef and rib steak and scrag of mutton".[50] Later still,[51] after "mutton" he adds further "and calfs pluck".

Perhaps the most interesting introduction of the specific through the mind of a character occurs in the penultimate episode. The type of advertisement represented by Plumtree's Potted Meat, which Bloom has twice condemned,[52] is cited as one which he would not use. The statement, in manuscript, concludes as follows: "The name on the label is Plumtree." After this sentence, Joyce adds: "A plumtree in a meatpot, registered trade mark."[53] Following this addition, the first galley proof contains the phrase "Beware of imitations.", after which Joyce adds further: "Plumtree."[54] We have here, at this stage, either a quotation from the advertisement[55] or a verbalized image of the label (either as reproduced in the advertisement or perhaps as attached to the pot). In a later galley Joyce replaces the newly introduced "Plumtree" with "Peatmot. Trumplee."[56] And between this second galley and publication, after "Trumplee." he must have added further: "Montpat. Plamtroo." In other words, the passage shifts ground, for the quotation from the advertisement or the visualization of the label, as the case may be, now ends with the warning "Beware of imitations.", and the words following represent specimen names of possible imitations which echo the name of the genuine product. These specimens, considered in themselves and especially in their context,[57] must be regarded as indirect quotation of Bloom's thought on the warning.

Not only does Joyce move from the general to the specific. In many revisions, he adds vivid picture-making details.

A number of these additions consist of single individualizing touches which vivify the hitherto undefined or vaguely realized. Bloom sees a boy smoking: "A smaller girl eyed him [the boy], listlessly holding her battered caskhoop." After "girl" Joyce adds "with scars of eczema on her forehead".[58]

Bloom passes "over a hopscotch court." Joyce deletes the period to add "with its forgotten pickeystone." [59]

"Horses with white frontlet plumes" come round a corner as Bloom is riding to Glasnevin. Joyce changes the "Horses" to "White horses".[60]

In another group of changes, Joyce introduces movement or heightens action already present. Bloom, in the butcher's shop, considers the nextdoor girl: "Strong pair of arms. Whacking a carpet on the clothesline. She does whack it, by George." Following this, Joyce adds: "The way her crooked skirt swings at each whack." [61]—giving us repeated motion. Shortly afterward, we read: "The crooked skirt swinging whack by whack by whack." [62] And later in the day, the thought of punishment reminds Bloom of "The crooked skirt swinging, whack by." [63]

Bloom visualizes: "Drinkers, drinking, laughed." Joyce deletes the period and adds "spluttering, their drink against their breath." [64]

In the library: "—Are you going, John Eglinton's eyebrows asked." Before "eyebrows" Joyce adds "active".[65]

The tale of Bloom's encounter with the Citizen is drawing to a close: "Begob he [the Citizen] made a swipe and let fly." After "he" Joyce adds "drew his hand and".[66]

Among Bloom's accusers we hear:

A FEMALE INFANT

And under Ballybough bridge?

Before "And" Joyce adds "(shakes a rattle)".[67]

Bloom's grandfather is described: "(*Profuse yellow spawn foaming over his bony epileptic lips.*)" Joyce alters the opening to read: "(*Agueshaken, profuse*".[68]

Bloom and Stephen observe a "star precipitated with great apparent velocity from Vega in the lyre above the zenith beyond the stargroup of the Tress of Berenice towards the zodiacal sign of Leo." After "velocity" Joyce adds "across the firmament"[69]—so that we now see the star against its background, without which the picture of its motion would be incomplete.

Molly remembers: "she [Mrs. Galbraith] was a lovely woman magnificent head of hair on her down to her waist like Kitty O'Shea". After "waist" Joyce adds "tossing it back like that".[70]

As may already have been observed, Joyce makes things present to various senses. Thus, Bloom looking toward his bath, "foresaw his pale body reclined in it at full, naked, oiled by scented melting soap, softly laved." After "naked," Joyce adds ", in a womb of warmth,"[71]—without which what bath of Bloom's could be complete?[72]

Another case in point follows an addition in which Joyce introduces into Molly's thought: "and when the priest was going by with the vatican to the dying blessing herself for his Majestad". After "with" he adds further "the bell bringing"[73]—and we hear as well as see.

In his desire to present reality as precisely, as specifically, and as vividly as possible, Joyce often abandons narrative for drama. This is true not only in part of the library episode[74] and in that welter of reality, the brothel scene, but also in many isolated passages which suddenly take flight, as it were, from the narrator's or the character's, mouth,[75] and present themselves independently.

Thus, Stephen recalls an early experience with water: "When I put my face into it in the basin at Clongowes. Out quickly, quickly." In this version, the second sentence may be read as Stephen's present narrative thought com-

pressed: 'I wished to take my face out of it very quickly.'
But between the two sentences Joyce inserts: "Can't
see! Who's behind me?" [76] Not only do these speeches
introduce straightforward, immediate dramatization, or
historical drama in the form of quotation; they also draw
into their orbit "Out quickly, quickly!", which can now
mean only one of two things: 'I wish to take my face out
of it quickly, quickly!' or, more urgently, 'Take it out
quickly, quickly!'

Bloom checks a didactic impulse: "Tell him if he smokes
he won't grow. O let him! His life isn't such a bed of
roses!" Following this, Joyce adds: "Waiting outside pubs
to bring da home. Come home to ma, da." [77] The speech
converts the scene into drama.

In church Bloom thinks: "Confession. Great weapon
in their hands." Between these sentences Joyce inserts:
"Everyone wants to. Then I will tell you all. Punish me,
please." [78]

Bloom goes on in the same vein: "Pray at an altar.
Flowers, incense, candles melting." Again, between these
sentences, Joyce inserts a dramatizing agent: "Hail Mary
and Holy Mary." [79] And there is more drama in the
context.[80]

Bloom is now thinking, characteristically, of the income
of the Church: "Bequests also: to say so many masses."
For the narrative "to say so many masses" Joyce substitutes a quotation from a specific bequest: "to the P. P.
for the time being in his absolute discretion. Masses for
the repose of my soul to be said publicly with open
doors." [81]

Soon afterward Bloom discovers that two buttons of his
waistcoat are open: "Women enjoy it. Never tell you."
Between these sentences Joyce inserts: "Annoyed if you
don't. Why didn't you tell me before." [82] Here, also, there
is more drama in the context.[83]

Bloom has just explained to Mrs. Breen why he is in
black: "Going to crop up all day, I foresee. Turn up like a
bad penny." Between these sentences Joyce adds: "Who's
dead, when and what did he die of?" [84]

Bloom recalls a nurse: "Old Mrs Thornton was a jolly old soul." Following this, Joyce adds: "Got her hand crushed by old Tom Wall's son. His first bow to the public. Head like a prize pumpkin." Then, before "Got" Joyce adds two dramatic specimens of the nurse's jolliness: "All my babies, she said. The spoon of pap in her mouth before she fed them. O, that's nyumnyum." [85] Interestingly enough, Bloom had once before presented Mrs. Thornton in her own words.[86] And we have already seen her enter the drama of the brothel.[87]

The sight of Sir Frederick Falkiner, recorder of Dublin, moves Bloom to think: "Old legal cronies cracking a magnum. I suppose he'd turn up his nose at that wine I drank." Between these sentences Joyce inserts: "Tales of the bench and assizer and annals of the bluecoat school. I sentenced him to ten years." [88]

Toward the close of the library scene Buck Mulligan chaffs Stephen for having attacked the work of Lady Gregory:

Couldn't you do the Yeats touch?
    He went on and down, changing with waving graceful arms:
    —I have conceived a play for the mummers, he said solemnly.

After "arms:" Joyce adds a dramatized specimen of the Yeats touch:

    —The most beautiful book that has come out of our country in my time. One thinks of Homer.[89]

The narrator of the *Cyclops* episode is discussing Blazes Boylan: "Dirty Dan the dodger's son that sold the same horses twice over to the government to fight the Boers. That's the bucko that'll organize her, take my tip." Between these sentences Joyce inserts: ". Old Whatwhat. I called about the poor and water rate, Mr Boylan. You what? The water rate, Mr Boylan. You whatwhat?" [90]

At twilight Bloom reflects: "Sad however because it lasts only a few years till they [girls] settle down to potwalloping and fuller's earth for the baby when ah ah."

After "potwalloping" Joyce adds "and papa's pants will soon fit Willy and".[91]

Shortly afterward, Bloom considers the plight of a Mrs. Duggan: "Husband rolling in drunk, stink of pub off him like a polecat. Have that in your nose all night, whiff of stale boose. Bad policy however to fault the husband." After the second sentence Joyce adds: ". Then ask in the morning: was I drunk last night?" [92]

In one change, a shift from the author's to a character's point of view represents a shift from narrative to dramatic presentation of the character's thought. Bloom thinks of the young student whose acquaintance Milly has made: "O well: she knows how to mind herself. But if not? No, nothing had happened. Of course it might. Wait in any case till it did." Joyce alters "had" to "has" and "did" to "does." [93] Apparently, Joyce had nodded into the conventional indirect mode of presenting thoughts, and here caught himself, as on another occasion he did not.[94]

Allied to all the aids to realism which I have thus far discussed—precision, specification, vividness, and dramatization—is Joyce's primal and unremitting interest in onomatopoeia.[95]

Stephen, in a passage which was part of an addition in a manuscript notebook containing an early version of the third episode, recalls a Parisian experience: "the barrier of the post office shut in your face by the usher." [96] In proof, Joyce fills this soundless memory with the clamor of the actual event as he alters the passage to read: "the banging door of the post office slammed in your face by the usher." [97]

In the same manuscript notebook, Joyce adds:

Listen: a fourworded wavespeech: seesoo, hrss, rsseeiss, oos. Vehement breath of water amid seasnakes, rearing horses, rocks. In cups of rocks it slops: flop, slop, slap; bounded in barrels. And spent, its speech ceases: it flows purling, wideflowing, floating foampool, flower unfurling.[98]

Bloom, in proof, considers the way women prepare a corpse for burial: "Huggermugger in corners. Then getting it ready." Between these sentences Joyce inserts: "Slop about in slipperslappers for fear he'd wake."[99]

On the way to Dignam's funeral, the carriage bearing Bloom stops to allow a drove of cattle to pass: "—Huuu! the drover's voice cried, his switch sounding on their flanks. Huuu out of that!" Joyce alters both "Huuu!" and "Huuu" to "Huuuh!"[100]—adding, with the aspirate, the final expulsion of breath which the prolonged cry necessitates.

At the cemetery, it occurs to Bloom that a gramophone might help one remember the dead: "Have a gramophone in every grave or keep it in the house. Remind you of the voice like the photograph reminds you of the face." Between these sentences Joyce introduces a dramatic performance:

> After dinner on a Sunday. Put on poor old greatgrandfather. Kraahraark! Hellohellohello amawfullyglad kraark awfullygladaseeagain hellohello amawf krpthsth.[101]

Almost immediately afterward, Bloom becomes aware of a rat by the noise it makes: "Ssld! A rattle of pebbles. Wait. Stop." Joyce changes "Ssld!", which is rather like a hiss, to "Rtststr!",[102] which bursts with "rattle" (itself felicitous for its inclusion of the animal's name) and ratness.

At the tale of Pyrrhus' failure to "retrieve the fortunes of Greece": "—Boohoo! Lenehan wept with a little noise." Following this, Joyce adds in proof: "Poor, poor, poor Pyrrhus!"[103] The whimpering explosive and the lugubrious vowel, effectively repeated, galvanize Lenehan's dream of passion. An entirely different effect is achieved in manuscript with the same explosive when, later in the day, Molly Bloom, "plump as a pouter pigeon", becomes "plump as a pampered pouter pigeon".[104]

In the Burton Restaurant Bloom sees a man at lunch: "Scoffing up stewgravy with bread." Before the last word Joyce inserts "sopping sippets of".[105] The added sibilants, reinforcing those already present, render the effect almost physically.

Another man in the Burton blows the froth from his

tankard: "Well up: it splashed yellow near his boot."
Following this, Joyce adds:

> A diner, knife and fork upright, elbows on table, ready for
> a second helping stared towards the foodlift. Other chap
> telling him something with his mouth full. Sympathetic
> listener. Table talk. I munched hum un thu Unchster
> Bunk un Munchday. Ha? Did you? [106]

Joyce's comment on an earlier mouthful is pertinent to
this one as well. The author is reading to Budgen from
the third episode:

> "Sir Lout's toys. Mind you don't get one bang on the
> ear. I'm the bloody well giant rolls all them bloody well
> boulders, bones for my steppingstones. Feefawfum. I
> zmells de bloodz oldz an Iridzman."
> Joyce read this with stammering, cluttered utterance,
> then stopped with a laugh at the odd sounds he made. . . .
> ". . . My Sir Lout [said Joyce] has rocks in his mouth
> instead of teeth. He articulates badly." [107]

Toward the close of the *Cyclops* episode, we hear of
the enraged Citizen cursing "bell book and candle in
Irish and Joe and little Alf trying to peacify him." After
"Irish" Joyce adds "spitting and spatting out of him".[108]

In the brothel scene, between REUBEN J's' "Nip the
first rattler." and a speech by Brother Buzz, Joyce must
have introduced, between the galley in which Brother
Buzz's words are added [109] and the Hanley proof, the
speech of

THE FIRE BRIGADE

Pflaap! [110]

Later in the same episode, Virag "*chases his tail.*)
Piffpaff! Popo! (*He stops, sneezes.*) Pchp!" Following
this, Joyce adds: "(*he worries his butt*) Prrrrrht!" [111]

The Croppy Boy, about to be hanged, has just said:

> I bear no hate to a living thing,
> But I love my country beyond the king.

The executioner, after a professional speech,

*jerks the rope, the croppy boy's tongue protrudes violently.
A violent erection of the hanged sends gouts of sperm
spouting through his death clothes on to the cobble
stones.*

Between these sentences Joyce adds closing and opening
parentheses respectively, and between the parentheses he
inserts:

THE CROPPY BOY
Horhot ho hray hor hother's hest [112]

The speech that is strangled with the young martyr is an
abbreviated version of a line in the ballad from which he
is quoting himself, as he echoes Benjamin Dollard's
performance of an earlier hour: [113] "And forgot to pray for
my mother's rest." [114]

As has been observed,[115] one form of innovation which
Joyce uses is distortion. In connection with personal
names, this takes the form of variation for purposes
suitable to given contexts. Two such variations introduced
in proof, create a desired atmosphere by sound effects.
At Stephen's explanation of Shakespeare's cuckoldry:
"—Cuckoo! Cuckoo! Buck Mulligan clucked lewdly. O
word of fear!" Joyce alters "Buck" to "Bird",[116] and,
later, "Bird" to "Cuck".[117]

Soon afterward, "Puck" Mulligan exclaims about John
Eglinton: "—O, the chinless Chinaman!" After this,
Joyce adds: "Chin Chon Eg Lin Ton." [118]

But Joyce's most interesting imitative contributions
are yet to come. In the brothel scene, Molly appears in
Turkish costume, beside her a camel: *"Fiercely she slaps
his haunch, scolding him in Moorish.)"* After *"haunch,"*
Joyce adds ", her goldcurb wristbangles angriling,".[119] The
vividly onomatopoeic verb (note the ting-a-ling of "angriling"; and the clash of "-bangles angril-", to get which
Joyce produces "wristbangles" on the analogy of *wrist-
bands*) is coined by conversion, *angrily* giving rise to
"angriling" as *almost* earlier gave rise to "almosting".[120]

A hunt is on. Simon Dedalus *"makes the beagle's call
giving tongue.)* Bulbul! Burblblbrurblbl! Hai, boy!" Al-

most directly afterward: "*The fox, brush pointed, runs swift, brighteyed, under the leaves. The crowd bawls of dicers, crown and anchor players, thimbleriggers, broadsmen*." Between these sentences Joyce inserts: "*The pack follows sniffing their quarry, beaglebaying, burblbrbling to be blooded*." [121] Here Joyce carries onomatopoeia through two stages. In Mr. Dedalus' speech he catches the beagle's cry; in the added stage direction, he converts the cry into a verb. By the same process he gives us the sound "Clipclap",[122] and verbifies it in "*Clipclaps*".[123]

But Joyce does not limit himself to sound effects. In order to imitate experiences as accurately as possible, he resorts to the use of rhythms. Thus, he once told Budgen that he had "been working hard all day" on two sentences:

> "You have been seeking the *mot juste?*" I [Budgen] said.
> "No," said Joyce. "I have the words already. What I am seeking is the perfect order of words in the sentence. There is an order in every way appropriate. I think I have it."
> "What are the words?" I asked.
> ". . . I am now writing the *Lestrygonians* episode, which corresponds to the adventure of Ulysses with the cannibals. My hero is going to lunch. But there is a seduction motive in the Odyssey, the cannibal king's daughter. Seduction appears in my book as women's silk petticoats hanging in a shop window. The words through which I express the effect of it on my hungry hero are: 'Perfume of embraces all him assailed. With hungered flesh obscurely, he mutely craved to adore.' You can see for yourself in how many different ways they might be arranged." [124]

On the same page in *Lestrygonians*, Bloom, in the Burton Restaurant, sees a "man spitting back on his plate: gristle: no teeth to chew it." Before "gristle" Joyce adds "halfmasticated", which prepares for his replacement of "chew" by "chewchewchew".[125] A hitherto inert statement now puts us vicariously, and vividly, through a dynamically realized process. And in this one change we have the shaping spirit of such other reduplicates as "riprippled",[126] "creecries",[127] "Clapclop. Clipclap. Clappyclap." [128] and "Clapclap. . . . Clappyclapclap. . . . Clapclipclap. . . . Clapclopclap." [129] and *"Clipclaps"*,[130] "gigglegiggled",[131] "spillspilling",[132] "Jigjag. Jigajiga. Jigjag.",[133] "pullpull",[134] and "curchycurchy".[135]

To revert to an earlier episode, the technique of a whole group of passages is illustrated by Joyce's treatment of Bloom in the jakes. The session with the old number of *Titbits* is on:

> Something new and easy. Our prize titbit. . . . He allowed his bowels to ease themselves quietly as he read, reading patiently that slight constipation of yesterday quite gone. . . . He glanced back through what he had read and envied kindly Mr Beaufoy who had written it and received payment of three pounds thirteen and six.

When Joyce has done revising, this passage reads:

> Something new and easy. No great hurry. Keep it a bit. Our prize titbit. . . . Quietly he read, restraining himself, the first column and, yielding but resisting, began the second. Midway, his last resistance yielding, he allowed his bowels to ease themselves quietly as he read, reading still patiently that slight constipation of yesterday quite gone. . . . He glanced back through what he had read and, while feeling his water flow quietly, he envied kindly Mr Beaufoy who had written it and received payment of three pounds thirteen and six.

Alternately interrupting identically timed themes, Joyce has caught with superb precision the effect of simultaneity. [136]

The evolution of a speech by Mulligan, in the library scene, further illustrates Joyce's sensitiveness to rhythm. Mulligan addresses Stephen in a parody of Synge:

> —It's what I'm telling you, mister honey, it's queer and sick we were, Haines and myself, the time himself brought it in. And we one hour and two hours and three hours in Connery's sitting civil waiting for pints apiece.

Between these sentences Joyce inserts:

'Twas murmur we did for a gallus potion would rouse a friar, I'm thinking, (laissez ici un espace suffisant pour six, sept paroles de la fin de la phrase) [137]

In a later galley for this passage, the space is left, and into it Joyce writes: "and he limp with leching." [138] What happened? I suspect that in the first galley, after bringing his sentence to the point at which he left it, Joyce felt that the rhythm of Synge's prose called for some such ending as he later formulated. The rhythm of the ending was perhaps running through his head. Perhaps even the construction (which occurs frequently in Molly Bloom's speech) had already been decided upon. But it may have refused at the time to take a verbal habitation. Therefore—to follow my suspicion through—Joyce left space for the words which should, and finally did, come.

In the afternoon, in manuscript, a "cavalcade in easy trot along Pembroke quay passed, outriders leaping gracefully in their saddles." [139] In proof, the phrase ends with "outriders leaping, leaping in their, in their saddles, in their saddles." Joyce deletes the first "their saddles". [140] Shortly afterward we hear: "In saddles of the leaders, leaping leaders, rode outriders." [141]

The rhythms of equitation engage Joyce again in the brothel scene. Bello "*thrusts out a figged fist and foul cigar.*) Here, kiss that. Both. Kiss." Following this, Joyce adds:

> (*he throws a leg astride and, squeezing with horseman's knees, calls in a hard voice*) Gee up! I'll ride him for the Eclipse stakes. (*he horserides ridehorse, leaping in the, in the saddle*). The lady goes a pace a pace and the coachman goes a trot a trot and the gentleman goes a gallop a gallop a gallop a gallop. [142]

Later in the same episode, in manuscript, "*Dwarfs ride them* [horses in a race], *rusty armoured, leaping in their, in their saddles.*" [143] In proof, the sentence ends: "*leaping, leaping in their, in their saddles.*"; [144] in the published version: "*leaping, leaping in their saddles.*"

Another type of prancing rhythm is employed in Molly's

monologue. Molly remembers Leopold, during their courtship,

> begging me to give him a tiny bit cut off my drawers . . .
> of course hes mad on the subject of drawers thats plain to
> be seen [etc.] . . . anything for an excuse to put his hand
> anear me drawers all the time till I promised to give him
> the pair off my doll to carry about in his waistcoat pocket

After the last "drawers" Joyce adds "drawers".[145]

In the Ormond Bar, Miss Douce addresses Lenehan:
"—You're the essence of vulgarity he [sic] said in
gliding." Joyce alters the ending to read: "she in gliding
said." [146]—giving us a keener sense of simultaneity of
speech and movement.

Blazes Boylan is about to leave the Ormond:

> —Wait a shake, begged Lenehan, drinking quickly, I
> wanted to tell you. Tom Rochford . . .
> —Come on to blazes, said Blazes Boylan, going.
> Lenehan gulped to go.
> —Got the horn or what? he said. Half a mo. I'm coming.

Joyce changes "Half a mo." to "Wait." [147] A man who is
drinking quickly and has just gulped to go is not likely to
waste words. What we now have, in Lenehan's dialogue, is
an audible quickening of pace. "Wait a shake" comes
down to "Wait."

Dollard is singing:

> —*When love absorbs my ardent soul* . . .
> —War! War! cried Father Cowley. You're the warrior.

Between these sentences Joyce inserts the following paragraph: "Roll of Bensoulbenjamin rolled to the quivery
loveshivery roofpanes." [148] By balanced repetition Joyce
has caught the rhythm of full rolling waves of sound
(Dollard is a bass baritone [149]) and of delicate answering
vibrations from the roofpanes.

While Dollard is singing, Bloom recalls:

> Night he ran round to us to borrow a dress suit for that
> concert. Trousers tight as a drum on him. Musical porkers.
> Molly did laugh when he went out. Threw herself back

across the bed, screaming, kicking. With all his belongings on show. O, saints above, I'm drenched! O, the women in the front row! O, I never laughed so much!

Joyce changes "much" to "many" [150]—and we can visualize Molly across the bed, screaming and kicking, gasping out, exhausted, or perhaps before suddenly going off into another transport, not a complete sentence, but an hysterical fragment. The rhythm of wild laughing speech is achieved by the characteristically abrupt interruption.

In the brothel scene, a moth flies *"Round and round"*.[151] At, and for, *"the everflying moth"* [152] (though here it "doth rest anon"), Virag recites:

> I'm a tiny thing
> Ever flying in the spring
> Round and round a ringaring.
> Long ago I was a king,
> Now I do this kind of thing
> On the wing, on the wing!
> Bing!

Joyce restores a "tiny" after "tiny" [153]—and the circularity of the moth's flight begins to make itself felt in the first line of the superbly appropriate utterance.

Between Bloom and Stephen's leavetaking, with "the lines of their valedictory arms, meeting at any point and forming any angle less than the sum of two right angles.", and the question "Alone, what did Bloom hear?", Joyce inserts:

> What sound accompanied the union of their tangent, the disunion of their (respectively) centrifugal and centripetal hands?
> The sound of the peal of the hour of the night by the chime of the bells in the church of Saint George.[154]

It is almost superfluous to remark on the chiming rhythm of "The sóund of the péal of the hóur of the níght by the chíme of the bélls in the chúrch of Saint Geórge." [155]

In the same episode, between Bloom's memory of the face of his father-in-law and a question concerning Molly's clothes, Joyce inserts:

What recurrent impressions of the same were possible by hypothesis?

Retreating, at the terminus of the Great Northern Railway, Amiens street, with constant uniform acceleration, along parallel lines meeting at infinity, if produced: along parallel lines, reproduced from infinity, with constant uniform retardation, at the terminus of the Great Northern Railway, Amiens street, returning.[156]

Comment on this passage is certainly superfluous.

At one point in Molly's reverie we hear: "wait by God he [Stephen] was on the cards this morning". Into the initial uncertainty of this memory Joyce introduces fluctuation: after "God" he adds "yes wait yes".[157] In a later proof he further curbs the tugging assertion by introducing, after "yes wait yes", "hold on".[158] And part of an addition in the context carries the uncertainty forward, with appropriately diminished force: "yes wait it all came out".[159]

In the numerous changes which we have thus far observed, Joyce, with some exceptions,[160] already has the words. But there are so many words that he does not have,[161] and consequently creates, that they merit separate treatment. These neologisms, as will become clear, increasingly adumbrate the style of *Finnegans Wake*, but I shall here treat them only as they bear upon the composition of *Ulysses*.

In coining his words, Joyce employs techniques of long standing. He extends the meaning of already existing words. Mulligan, after shaving, "with stroking fingers felt the smooth skin." After "stroking" Joyce adds "palps of".[162] The only current meaning for the noun *palp* is the zoological 'palpus' or 'feeler.'[163] Yet it is understandable that the word should be applied to the tip of the finger, with which one *palpates*.

Composition, ubiquitous in *Ulysses*, inspires a number of changes. Two or more already existing words, in combination, often achieve, besides the compactness to be expected, a wider radius of suggestiveness, a stronger sense of identification or of simultaneity, than their components had. Two specimens which I have presented in another connection are introduced when Dollard's voice "rolled to the quivery loveshivery roofpanes." [164] On the analogy of such words as *love-smitten* and *love-fond*, Joyce gives us not only "loveshivery" but also "love-soft"; [165] while "roofpanes" follows the model of *roof-windows*.

At twilight, Bloom thinks: "O sweety all your little white up I saw dirty girl". So reads the passage in galley, but between this galley [166] and a later proof, "white" becomes "girlwhite".[167] And Joyce also coins "Girlgold".[168]

In the brothel, a dog "*growls, his scruff standing, a gobbet of pig's knuckle between his molars.*" Joyce fills in his picture by deleting the period and adding "through which rabid scumspittle dribbles." [169] Here, again, there are analogues, in *scum-board* and *scum-soap*.

Before Bloom and Stephen part at the end of the day, they stand silent, "each contemplating the other in both mirrors of the flesh of fellowfaces." Before the final word Joyce inserts "his nothis".[170] Later the newly added words give way to "theirhisnothis".[171]

The bells of St. George's Church chime, Stephen walks off, and Bloom, "Alone," feels the "cold of interstellar space . . . the incipient intimations of proximate dawn." Following this, Joyce adds: "Of what did bellchime and handtouch and footstep and lonechill remind him?" [172] In this instance, the coinage, "lonechill", bringing up the rear of a line of already current compounds, comes upon us in a receptive, even expectant state.

But Joyce does not only combine already existing words; he also extends their use—again, as in previous instances,[173] by conversion. Simon Dedalus "took off his silk hat and, blowing out impatiently his bushy moustache, began to rake through his hair with his fingers." For "began to rake through" Joyce substitutes "welsh-combed".[174] Before this change *Welsh comb* had only one meaning: 'the thumb and four fingers.' [175] With the dual function of *comb* to encourage him, and on the analogy of such a word as *Christian-name*, Joyce converts the compound noun into a compound verb. By the same process he verbifies *"Easter kiss"* [176] in *"Easterkissing".*[177]

Besides compounds, Joyce also creates by analogy single words. In the penultimate episode we learn that Bloom was once prevented from completing a song, in part, by "oscillation between events of imperial and of local interest, the diamond jubilee of Queen Victoria (born 1820, acceded 1837) and the opening of the new municipal fish market:". Thus the second of three available proofs [178] for this passage. In the third, Joyce introduced "anticipated" before "diamond" and, in its wake, "posticipated" before "opening".

And now for the type of neologism which, based upon "an occasional mode of word formation," [179] ultimately carried Joyce farthest from the current language. Specimens of blending in *Ulysses* are plentiful; and a number of them were added late. In an addition already cited, the simple statement 'I met him in the Ulster Bank on Monday' is chewed into "I munched hum un thu Unchster Bunk un Munchday." [180]

"John Eglinton", before mentioning the views of two Shakespeareans, becomes "John Eclecticon." [181] And we have already seen this Irishman Orientalized as "Chin Chon Eg Lin Ton." [182]

In the brothel scene, Virag says: "Insects of the day spend their brief existence in reiterated coition, lured by the smell of the inferiorly pulchritudinous fumale Pretty Poll!" After the appropriate "fumale" Joyce adds "possessing extendified pudendal nerve in dorsal region." [183] Between proof and publication, "pudendal nerve" becomes, pertinently, "pudendal verve".[184]

Near the close of the same episode, Corny Kelleher, after rescuing Stephen from the watch, is leaving the scene:

> *With thumb and palm Corny Kelleher reassures that the two bobbies will allow the sleep to continue for what else is to be done. With a slow nod Bloom conveys his gratitude as that is exactly what Stephen needs. The car jingles round the corner of the lane. Corny Kelleher again re-*

*assures with his hand. Bloom with his hand assures Corny
Kelleher that he is reassured. The tinkling hoofs and
jingling harness grow fainter.*

After *"jingles"* and before *"lane"* Joyce adds *"tooraloom"*;
he changes the second *"reassures"* to *"reassuralooms"*,
"assures" to *"assuralooms"*, and *"reassured"* to *"reassuraloomtay"*; after *"fainter"* he deletes the period to add
"with their tooralooloo looloo ay." [185] And between this
galley and publication, the last addition becomes *"with
their tooralooloo looloo lay."* [186] Joyce first introduces
simultaneity by alternating two themes (a device we have
already met [187]), the movement of the car and Kelleher's
lilting. Then, apparently, observing the vowel sound common to *"reassures"*, *"assures"*, *"reassured"*, and *"tooraloom"*, he builds up a series of blends that synchronize
even more closely the gestures of assurance and the
lilting, which he carries forward. His perception of the
common vowel would not surprise us under ordinary
circumstances, and it surprises us not at all here, since,
before the car jingles off, Kelleher has sung his *tooraloom*
no less than ten times,[188] and Bloom has thought it at him
twice,[189] as well as sung it four times on his own.[190] The
coincidence of four occurrences of the root *-sure-* with
the character responsible for all these *tooraloom's*, and
those just added,[191] undoubtedly set off Joyce's amal-
gamating impulse. And the impulse goes on to telescope
Kelleher's last recital, the third of this particular snatch,
in the last added blend. To put it mathematically, "tooralooloo looloo" equals "tooraloo-" plus "-loo-" plus "-loo-"
plus "-loo-" of "With my tooraloom tooraloom tooraloom
tooraloom." [192] The final *"lay"* brings up the rear with a
blend of "tay" [193] and *lay* (in the sense of 'song'), as the
liquid follows up its line of predecessors.

In one passage we may watch a pair of blends in
process of formation. The catechism reads:

> Did they [Bloom and Stephen] find their educational
> careers similar?
> Bloom had passed successively through a dame's school

and the high school; Stephen through the preparatory, junor, middle and senior grades of the intermediate and through the matriculation, first arts and degree courses of University.

For "Bloom had" Joyce substitutes "If Stephen had been Bloom he would have"; for "Stephen", "if Bloom had been Stephen he would have passed successively".[194] With the hypothetical interchange of identities, the stage is set, for later Joyce points up the interchange by blending the names of the characters through the transposition of initial consonants (a device which he has used before[195]). The answer becomes:

> Substituting Stephen for Bloom Stoom would have passed successively through a dame's school and the high school. Substituting Bloom for Stephen Blephen would have passed successively [etc.][196]

Joyce has thus come a long way from the simple interest in orthodox precision which I discussed at the opening of this essay. In effect, he has travelled the whole road from *Dubliners* to *Finnegans Wake*. Even in *Ulysses*, he crosses established borders. And though his excursions are still relatively infrequent, he is clearly moving toward the full adoption of what one critic, quoting *Ulysses*, has described as the language of the outlaw.[197]

ii

Joyce's revisions represent almost exclusively a process of elaboration. Great numbers of additions gravitate into patterned constellations of purpose and method, and innumerable details, in the final text as well as in the additions, become luminous with meaning.

In the matter of style, Joyce is extraordinarily alert to the possibilities of greater success in the achievement of a multitude of effects.

His primary concern is for realistic representation. To this end he adds continually, rare lapses notwithstanding, precision in the use of words, specification, vividness, dramatization, onomatopoeia, and rhythms. In these efforts, as I have suggested, we may trace his development from *Dubliners* to *Finnegans Wake*.

But to Joyce style means far more than realistic representation. In his quest for the perfect union of matter and manner, he evolves a variety of techniques for a variety of episodes. In the process of revision, he intensifies the incubism of the graveyard, the journalistic atmosphere of the newspaper office, the gastronomic effects of lunch, the Elizabethan wrapping around the discussion of Shakespeare, the musical properties of the Ormond Bar, the language of the pub. He heightens the sentimental aura around Gerty MacDowell, as also the accompanying rhythm of tumescence and detumescence, the 'embryonic development' of English style for the lying-in, the jerky rhythm appropriate to the brothel, the climate of exhaustion which envelops the cabman's shelter, the cold impersonality of the penultimate episode, the turning movement of the throbbing final episode.

Briefly, the revisions afford a direct view into the mind of Joyce in the process of creation. This insight, fascinating in itself as an adventure in psychological analysis, yields two contributions of critical importance. By making us aware of fresh and dominant relationships, it enables us to effect a fuller synthesis in our apprehension of the finished work of art. By making clearer the kinship of that work with Joyce's earlier and later works, it enables us to appraise more justly Joyce's total achievement.

ABBREVIATIONS

(for Chapters 5–7)

Editions of ULYSSES

S *Ulysses*, Paris, Shakespeare and Co., February, 1922.
The first edition, set up from the proof sheets treated
in the present study.

EP *Ulysses*, published for The Egoist Press, London, by
John Rodker, Paris, October, 1922. All citations from
this the first English edition (struck off from the
original plates) take account of the seven pages of
errata laid in.

S4 *Ulysses*, Paris, Shakespeare and Co., fourth printing,
January, 1924. All citations from this edition take
account of the list of "Additional corrections" on
pp. 733–36.

S6 *Ulysses*, Paris, Shakespeare and Co., sixth printing,
August, 1925. All citations from this edition take
account of the list of "Additional corrections" on
pp. 733–36. Both the text and the list, in all passages
for which I cite this edition, are identical with those
of S4.

S9 *Ulysses*, Paris, Shakespeare and Co., ninth printing,
May, 1927. This edition follows that of May, 1926,
for which the type was entirely reset. The "Additional corrections" mentioned under S4 and S6 were,
with some exceptions, incorporated.

U *Ulysses*, New York, Random House, sixth printing,
February, 1934. This edition is based upon a corrupt

pirated text. The publishers included it in the Modern Library—after the exposure of their mistake. Since, however, it is the only edition generally available to American readers, I am compelled to use it for citation from the final text. Whenever, in collating editions, I mention *U*, I do so for the convenience of the reader, not for authority. [N.B. The 1961 printing, which describes itself as a "NEW EDITION, CORRECTED AND RESET," appeared too late for consideration here.]

In citing from *Ulysses*, whatever the edition, for the sake of complete accuracy I give all opening and closing punctuation marks as in the text quoted and place outside the quotations all opening and closing punctuation marks that are mine. In citing the Random House edition, I refer to it as *U*, following it directly with the page number, e.g., *U*5.

OP   *Ulysses*, 2 vols., Hamburg-Paris-Bologna, Odyssey Press, third impression, August, 1935. The first impression of this edition called itself the "definitive standard edition . . . specially revised, at the author's request, by *Stuart Gilbert*." In the second impression, the text was made more accurate. For the superiority of the third impression to the first two, see J. F. Spoerri, "The Odyssey Press Edition of James Joyce's 'Ulysses,'" *Papers of the Bibliographical Society of America*, L (Second Quarter, 1956), 195–98.

I owe some of the information used above to R. F. Roberts, "Bibliographical Notes on James Joyce's 'Ulysses,'" *Colophon*, New Series, I (Spring, 1936), 565–79.

Manuscript and Other Materials

B   Manuscripts of parts of *Ulysses* exhibited at the Librairie La Hune, Paris, in 1949 and acquired by the Lockwood Memorial Library of the University of

Buffalo. Numbers following the symbol *B* will refer
to entries in the La Hune catalogue *James Joyce: sa
vie, son œuvre, son rayonnement* (Paris, 1949),
items 252–53, 255–59. (Item 254 was reportedly lost
in transit between Paris and Buffalo.) These manuscripts are also described in John J. Slocum and
Herbert Cahoon, A *Bibliography of James Joyce*
[1882–1941] (New Haven, 1953), E5b.

H   Proof sheets of *Ulysses* described by Slocum and
Cahoon, E5f, quoting the private catalogue of Edward W. Titus as follows: "Complete and final
proofs of the first edition of this stupendous work
with the author's profuse autograph corrections,
emendations and additions exceeding sometimes 160
words on a single page. These important additions
are not found in the manuscript of the work, that
had been the sensation of the memorable Quinn
Sale in 1924." Made available to me by Mr. T. E.
Hanley and now in the University of Texas Library.

I   Miles L. Hanley and others, *Word Index to James
Joyce's Ulysses* (Madison, Wisconsin, 1937). A list
of "Errata in Random House Edition" occurs on
pp. xiii–xix.

R   Manuscript of *Ulysses* made available to me by the
late A. S. W. Rosenbach and now in the Rosenbach
Foundation. Described in Slocum and Cahoon, E5a,
quoting the catalogue of the Quinn sale, no. 4936:
"Original autograph manuscript of 'Ulysses,' written
on over 1200 pages."—etc.

W   Proof sheets of *Ulysses* made available to me by
Miss Marian G. Willard and now in the Houghton
Library of Harvard University. Miss Sylvia Beach,
publisher of the first edition of *Ulysses*, described
this material as follows: "A complete set, and several
incomplete sets of the proofs abundantly corrected
and added to by the author. About 600 pages con-

tain 5 to 10 lines of autograph corrections, others are almost completely covered with manuscript.

"These proofs show the important changes that James Joyces [sic] made in his 'Ulysses' while it was printing, and his manner of continually adding text to successive sets of proofs up to the very moment before going to press."—*Catalogue of a Collection Containing Manuscripts & Rare Editions of James Joyce* . . . (Paris, 1935), p. 3.

Miss Willard numbered the galleys from 1 to 212. The pagination of the galleys underwent so many changes that it seems best to refer to the pages of each galley by a fresh count. A specimen reference follows: W187:4 indicates galley numbered 187, fourth page.

1—James Joyce: A Study in Words

1. Frank Budgen, *James Joyce and the Making of ULYSSES* (New York, 1934), p. 57. Cf. *Dubliners* (New York, 1926), Introduction by Padraic Colum, pp. viii–ix.

2. New York, 1928.   3. New York, 1934.

4. *Portrait*, p. 2.

5. Seán O'Faoláin, "The Cruelty and Beauty of Words," *Virginia Quarterly Review*, IV (April 1928), 221.

6. *Portrait*, p. 3.   7. *Ibid.*, p. 6.   8. *Ibid.*, p. 11.

9. *Ibid.*, p. 60.   10. *Dubliners*, p. 7.

11. *Portrait*, pp. 126–27.   12. *Ibid.*, p. 176.

13. *Ulysses*, p. 5.   14. *Portrait*, p. 191.

15. *Ibid.*, pp. 193–94.   16. *Ibid.*, pp. 207–8.

17. *Ibid.*, p. 209.   18. *Ibid.*, p. 221.

19. *Work in Progress*, in book form for sale, has appeared in the following fragments: *Anna Livia Plurabelle* (New York, 1928), *Tales Told of Shem and Shaun* (Paris, 1929), *Haveth Childers Everywhere* (Paris and New York, 1930), *Two Tales of Shem and Shaun* (London, 1932), *The Mime of Mick, Nick and the Maggies* (The Hague, 1934), *Storiella as She Is Syung* (London, 1937). [The completed work appeared as *Finnegans Wake* (London and New York, 1939) after the original publication of this essay.]

20. *Ulysses*, p. 85.   21. *Othello*, I.i.13.

22. *Ulysses*, p. 68.   23. *Ibid.*, p. 86.   24. *Ibid.*, p. 239.

25. *Ibid.*, p. 245.

26. Cf. E. A. Abbott, *A Shakespearian Grammar* (London and New York, 1891), p. 5.

27. *Ulysses*, p. 47.   28. Budgen, p. 54.

29. Stuart Gilbert, *James Joyce's ULYSSES* (London, 1930), p. 39.   30. *Ulysses*, p. 122.   31. *Ibid.*, p. 115.

32. *Ibid.*, p. 116.   33. *Ibid.*, p. 48.   34. Budgen, p. 55.   35. *Ulysses*, p. 388.   36. *Ibid.*, p. 55.   37. *Ibid.*, p. 112.

38. *Ibid.*, pp. 535, 536, 539. "Poulaphouca" Joyce owes to the name of a waterfall; cf. p. 535.   39. *Ibid.*, p. 85.

40. *Ibid.*, pp. 166–67.   41. *Ibid.*, p. 175.

42. *Ibid.*, p. 271.   43. *Ibid.*, p. 273.

44. *Anna Livia Plurabelle*, Fragment of *Work in Progress* (London, 1930), p. 32.

45. "From a Banned Writer to a Banned Singer," *Hound & Horn*, II (July 1932), 543.

46. *Portrait*, pp. 67–68.

47. Aldous Huxley, ed., *The Letters of D. H. Lawrence* (New York, 1932), p. 750.   48. *Ulysses*, p. 120.

49. Budgen, p. 205.

50. G. V. L. Slingsby, "Writes a Common Reader," in Samuel Beckett *et al., Our Exagmination Round his Factification for Incamination of Work in Progress* (Paris, 1929), p. 189.   51. Gilbert, p. 205.

2—Stephen Hero

1. The 1955 edition of *Stephen Hero* incorporates the text of twenty-five additional manuscript pages, edited with a foreword by John J. Slocum and Herbert Cahoon. The text of five more pages of manuscript is made available by Slocum and Cahoon in Marvin Magalaner, ed., *A James Joyce Miscellany: Second Series* (Carbondale [Illinois], 1959), and in the 1963 edition of *Stephen Hero*. For first publication of the original version of the *Portrait*, a brief narrative essay antecedent to *Stephen Hero*, see R. M. Kain and R. E. Scholes, eds., "The First Version of Joyce's 'Portrait,'" *Yale Review*, XLIX (1960), 355–69.

3—Homer's Odyssey and Joyce's Ulysses

1. *James Joyce's ULYSSES* (New York, 1934).

2. Frank Budgen, *James Joyce and the Making of*

ULYSSES (New York, 1934), p. 15.

3. Cf. Gilbert, pp. 27–28 and Part II.

4. In *The Odyssey of Homer*, tr. S. H. Butcher and A. Lang (Modern Library ed.).

5. *Ulysses* (New York, 1934), p. 5.

6. *Ibid.*, p. 7. This cry at the opening of *Ulysses* recurs at its close in Molly Bloom's "the sea the sea" (p. 768).

7. Gilbert, p. 99, mentions the passage from *Ulysses* in another connection.

8. My numbers refer only to newly discovered parallels.

9. Cf. *Odyssey*, p. 134, his reply to Polyphemus' question about the location of his ship; p. 136, his offering of wine; p. 137, his anonymity (cf. *Ulysses*, p. 712, for use of "Noman"); p. 141, his refusal to return at Polyphemus' invitation.

10. Cf. *Odyssey*, pp. 165, 185, for the words of Teiresias and Circe. This is at least the second misrepresentation of Odysseus to his men. Cf. also p. 185 for a twisted report of Circe's instructions with regard to the Sirens ("me only she bade listen") and p. 182 ("if thou thyself art minded to hear").

11. *Ulysses*, p. 424. See also p. 434, the Bawd's first speech; p. 491, Zoe drawing Bloom over the threshold.

12. *Ibid.*, p. 491. See also p. 429: "Probably lost cattle. Mark of the beast."

13. *Ibid.*, p. 443. Cf. p. 467, the Oriental music; p. 491, the musicroom.

14. *Ibid.*, p. 620. For the factual basis of Odysseus' yarn, compare *Odyssey*, p. 193 ("But now . . . of returning.") with *ibid.*, p. 218 ("But when . . . their return.").

15. *Ibid.*, pp. 313–14. For a dream of Penelope's, see p. 308.

4—*Local Allusions in* Ulysses

1. (London: Mellifont Press Ltd., n.d.). Not very long ago, the Reference Department of the Wayne University Library could not locate a copy for interlibrary loan in the United States.

2. *Ulysses*, Modern Library ed. (copyright 1942), p. 101.

3. See T. C. Croker, *Popular Songs of Ireland* (London, n.d.), pp. 158–64.

4. H. R. Hayward, ed., *Ulster Songs and Ballads of the Town and the Country* (London [1925]), pp. 47–48. Stuart Gilbert, *James Joyce's ULYSSES: A Study* (New York, 1930), p. 178, lists "your Cork legs are running away with you" as a "Hibernicism."   5. Croker, p. 230.

6. For text and discussion of the song, see *ibid.*, pp. 230–37. The song is played in *Ulysses*, p. 581.

7. *Ulysses*, p. 306. The Modern Library edition's "synanthropy" is corrupt; see the Odyssey Press "definitive standard edition" (Hamburg, Paris, Bologna, 1932), p. 323.

8. *Ulysses*, p. 346. My comment was written independently of Arland Ussher, *Three Great Irishmen: Shaw, Yeats, Joyce* (London, 1952), p. 124 n.

9. Title of Yeats's essay on Moran in *The Celtic Twilight* (London, 1893), pp. 67–80.

10. F. N. Robinson, ed., *The Complete Works of Geoffrey Chaucer* (Boston, etc. [1933]), p. 818.

11. Mr. Gilbert has very kindly given me permission to quote his letter. In August, 1953, I heard from another source that the "waxies' Dargle" was held in Ringsend, Dublin, and was so called because it was the cobblers' equivalent of fashionable parties held on the Powerscourt estate in the Glen of the Dargle.

12. (New York, 1952), p. 29.

5—Stephen Dedalus

[For an explanation of the abbreviations used, see Abbreviations preceding Notes.]

1. *The Little Review*, V (January, 1919, and February–March, 1919).

2. Frank Budgen, *James Joyce and the Making of ULYSSES* (New York, 1934), p. 105.   3. U17.

4. *A Portrait of the Artist as a Young Man* (New York, 1928), p. 229.   5. *Ibid.*, p. 100. Italics mine.

6. U46. Italics mine.   7. Page 2.   8. U664.

9. *Portrait*, p. 298.   10. U51.

11. Cf. *Portrait*, p. 205: "His mind, in the vesture of a doubting monk, . . . lurking-place"; pp. 224–25: "His fellow student's rude humour ran like a gust through the cloister of Stephen's mind, . . . whispering two and two behind their hands"; p. 258: "I was born to be a monk. — . . . A monk! His own image started forth a profaner of the cloister" etc.; p. 260: "a priest of the eternal imagination" etc.   12. *Ibid.*, p. 283.   13. U205.   14. U5.

15. U512.   16. *Ibid.*   17. U48.   18. U203.

19. *Portrait*, p. 245.   20. *Ibid.*, pp. 193–94.   21. U628.

22. U28.   23. U205.   24. U566.   25. Page 285.

26. U133.   27. U546.

28. U547. Cf. *Portrait*, pp. 51–64.   29. U192.

30. Page 250.

31. *James Clarence Mangan*—reprinted from *St. Stephen's* (Dublin), May, 1902—(London [1930]), p. 9. The essay is also available in Patricia Hutchins, *James Joyce's Dublin* [London, 1950], pp. 57–59; *National Student* (Dublin), no. 114 (March 1952), 9–12; *James Joyce Review*, I (Feb. 2, 1957), 31–38, and *The Critical Writings of James Joyce*, ed. Ellsworth Mason and Richard Ellmann (New York, 1959), pp. 73–83. Mason and Ellmann publish a translation of the manuscript of a lecture in Italian on Mangan, dated 1907, in which Joyce uses Shelley's phrase once again (*ibid.*, p. 182).   32. U208.

33. Pages 196–97. The words "Fabulous artificer . . . hawklike man" echo the earlier passage.

34. U214–15.   35. Pages 263–65.   36. U168.   37. U96.

38. U309, 392, 402, 457, 664, 737, 757.   39. U41.

40. U208.   41. U493.

42. Regarding the epiphanies, see James Joyce, *Stephen Hero*, ed. Theodore Spencer, John J. Slocum, and Herbert Cahoon [New York, 1955], pp. 210 ff; regarding the whetstones, *ibid.*, p. 36, especially the following: "Stephen found Maurice [his brother] very useful for raising objections."

43. James Joyce, *Epiphanies*, ed. O. A. Silverman (Buffalo, 1956).   44. U143; W46:6.   45. U195; W57:3.

46. Page 236.   47. U147.   48. U142; W44:5.

49. U544; W128:6. The schoolhouse version of the rid
dle (U27) and its answer (U28—echoed on pp. 47, 545
557) are variants on a version recorded by P. W. Joyce
English as We Speak It in Ireland (London & Dublin
1910), p. 187.

50. U682–83; W171:4. The rest of the text was intro
duced in H.

For other parodies of Catholic ritual by Stephen, cf
U424, 512–13.

51. U201; W59:1. In this galley Joyce also adds "An
tiquity mentions" before "That" and the just-revealing
"slight" before "concern".   52. W60:1.

53. U674; W174:5. Then, following "quasisensations"
Joyce adds "of concealed identities". Bloom's auditive
quasisensation, left unrecorded here, was introduced in H

54. Cf. U186, Stephen's thought: "Local colour. Work
in all you know."   55. U55–56.   56. U86 ff.

57. U19. I corrects U's "fifty-five" to "fiftyfive".

58. U203; W59:2. A few pages back Joyce anticipated
this addition when, to the first phrase in Stephen's
thought: "His private papers. *Ta an bad ar an tir. Tain*
[sic] *imo shagart.*" he appended "in the original." (U192
W55:8) Stephen's private thought thus attains to an
ostentatious expression at the round table.

In W59:2 Joyce also introduces "new" before "Vien
nese", unobtrusively dating the speech.

He must have introduced "gorbellied" before "works'
between W60, a later galley covering this passage, and H
in which it appears already incorporated in the text. Very
likely echoing *I Henry IV*, II, ii, 92, this insertion adds to
the Elizabethan atmosphere of the library scene.

59. U203–4; W59:3. Joyce must have introduced "loos
ing her nightly waters on the jordan" between W60, a
later galley covering this passage, and H, in which it ap
pears already incorporated in the text.

Robert M. Adams, *Surface and Symbol: The Consist
ency of James Joyce's ULYSSES* (New York, 1962), p
127, writes: "The curious titles of the tracts . . . are
anachronistic to the seventeenth century . . . and in fact

they are not of that period at all. Joyce derived them from a review article based on Octave Delepierre's *History of the Literature of Lunatics;* the article appeared in the *Irish Independent* of June 15, 1904, p. 4, and Joyce used nothing else in it."

60. *U*383; B258A, p. 7.

61. W108:6. The proof reads: "out of her bosom" and "Virgillius". The rest of the text must have been introduced between this galley and H, in which it appears already incorporated.

OP: "Virgilius"

62. *U*386; W109:1. In H, Joyce corrected "bribered" to "bridebed".

63. *U*394–95; R and W109:8, respectively. A. M. Klein, "The Oxen of the Sun," *Here and Now*, I (January 1949), 45, says of this passage: "it gets all its terms mixed up."

64. *U*636; W154:8. Here, also, Joyce changes "said" to "ejaculated".

65. The last line of the chorus runs as follows: "From Ushant to Scilly is thirty-five leagues." The third stanza begins:

The first land we made it is known as the Deadman,
Next Ram Head near Plymouth, Start, Portland, and Wight;

Thomas Wood, ed., *The Oxford Song Book* (London, etc., 1927), II, 77. The song has a number of variants: cf. L. A. Smith, *The Music of the Waters* (London, 1888), p. 63; S. Baring-Gould, *English Minstrelsie* (Edinburgh, 1895), III, 56–58; W. B. Whall, *Sea Songs and Shanties* (Glasgow, 1927), pp. 15–16; C. J. Sharp, *English Folk Songs* (London, n.d.), II, 97–99.

66. Cf. Stuart Gilbert, *James Joyce's ULYSSES: A Study* (New York, 1952), p. 41.

67. *U*16; W5:6.   68. H.   69. Cf. Gilbert, *ibid.*

70. *U*28; W9:4.

71. *U*43; B253, p. 8. R like *U*: "wonders, what? Missionary to Europe after fiery".

72. *U*183; W53:8.   73. *Ibid.*

74. U383; W108:6. After "But" Joyce adds ",gra-mercy,". 75. U192; W56:8. 76. U22, 195. 77. U194.

78. U197; W57:4.

79. U196; W57:4. Regarding the problem of identity in Joyce, see Rudolf Hentze, *Die proteïsche Wandlung im "Ulysses" von James Joyce* (Marburg, 1933), pp. 4–27.

80. U142; W44:5. 81. U246. 82. U143. 83. *Ibid.*

84. U190. 85. U212.

86. A telescoping and adaptation of two lines from the ballad "The Wearin' o' the Green":

I met wid Napper Tandy, and he took me by the hand,
And he said, 'How's poor ould Ireland, and how does she
    stand?'

John Cooke, ed., *The Dublin Book of Irish Verse* (Dublin and London, 1924), p. 743. Earlier in the day Stephen had adapted the first line to the exiled Egan, thus: "He takes me, Napper Tandy, by the hand." (*U45*)

87. U580; W132:5. To preclude repetition, he changes the opening to read: "(*She keens with banshee woe.*)"

The inspiration for the addition regarding "poor old Ireland" lies undoubtedly in the earlier juxtaposition of "Silk of the kine and poor old woman" (p. 15). Both phrases are symbols for Ireland.

88. U629; W153:2. Here, also, "a half" is added before "laugh".

89. U650; W178:1. Joyce inserts "ecclesiastical celi-bacy," in W176:1. 90. See above, n. 59.

91. U48. In B253, p. 15, Joyce makes his way to the final choice of "vampire" through the following delibera-tions: "the pale vampire [canceled], bat [canceled] vam-pire,".

The last two sentences quoted are the products of much more deliberation. B *ibid.* reads: "His lips lipped and mouthed fleshless lips of air: Mouth to her moongmbh [canceled] moombh". In the margin Joyce writes:

> moongb [canceled]
> moongmbwb   [canceled]
> moongbm [canceled]

```
        moongmb
        moongbhmb
        moongb [canceled]
        moongmbhb
        moongbh
        moombh
```

After "moombh" in the text Joyce inserts: "Oomb, tombwombing tomb south. His mouth moulded breath, un-
speeched, oo to ah, roar of cataractic planets, balled globed
blazing, roaring wayawayawayawayaway." Then he replaces "tombwombing" with "allwombing" and "oo to
ah" with "oo, ee, eh, ah", and deletes "balled". (Very
likely allied is the marginal note "a.e.i.o.u" next to the
preceding paragraph, which begins: "Here.") R represents
a further stage in the process: "His lips lipped and
mouthed fleshless lips of air: mouth to her woomb. Oomb,
allwombing tomb. His mouth moulded issuing breath, un-
speeched: ooeeehah: roar of cataractic planets, globed,
blazing, roaring wayawayawayawayaway." H, like U, reads
"womb" and "wayawayawayawayaway".

   92. U131; W38:1. With Stephen's quatrain, cf. Doug-
las Hyde, "My Grief on the Sea," *Love Songs of Con-
nacht* (London and Dublin, 1895), p. 31:

> And my love came behind me—
>   He came from the South;
> His breast to my bosom,
> His mouth to my mouth.

Hyde's book is mentioned in U184, 196.

   93. U136–37. U's "pentitent" is corrected by I.

   94. W45:1. The vampire's kiss is last heard of as one of
the methods of impregnation which Stephen discusses at
the lying-in hospital: "bigness wrought . . . by potency
of vampires mouth to mouth". (U383)

   95. The whole addition is "said, whose works are probably", but Joyce deletes the last four words. R reads: "Antisthenes, pupil of Gorgias, Stephen said, took the palm
of beauty from Kyrios Menelaus' broodmare, Helen, and

handed it to poor Penelope." Here, before "Helen" Joyc
inserts "Argive".

96. U198–99; W57:6. In the next galley (W58:6
Joyce substitutes "brooddam" for "broodmare".

97. U147.

98. U554; W129:7. This addition is made after Joyc
has added, also here: "Forget not Madam Grissel Steeven
nor the suine scions of the house of Lambert. And Noal
was drunk with wine. And his ark was open."

The mocking equation between Pasiphae's wooden co
and the confession box further expresses Stephen's an
mus against the Church. For an earlier equation with th
confession box, cf. *Stephen Hero*, p. 209: "Father Jacl
in-the-Box."

Random's "Passiphae" is an erratum. Cf. OP.

99. In the train of *grandoldgrossfather*, Joyce later pr
duces "Besterfarther" (*Finnegans Wake*, p. 414), which
Michael Stuart has noted, is based upon the Norwegia
for 'grandfather.' ("Mr. Joyce's Word-Creatures," *Sympc
sium*, II [October 1931], 464)

100. Page 299. Perhaps this very passage inspired th
Gaelic loan. On the other hand, Stephen may owe th
loan, as he does another, to a grammar which, according t
Stephen Hero (p. 56), he once studied. *Sean-atair* occur
in the Reverend Eugene O'Growney's *Simple Lessons i
Irish*, Part III (Dublin, 1906), p. 24.

The other loan is made in the library scene, whe
Stephen thinks: "His private papers in the original. *Ta a
bad ar an tir. Tiam imo shagart.*" (U192. *Tiam* is an e
ratum for *Taim*—cf. n. 58, above, and OP.) The firs
Gaelic sentence ('The boat is on the land') occurs almos
verbatim in O'Growney's *Simple Lessons in Irish*, Part
(Dublin, 1909), p. 22. The early exercises in this gramma
swarm with statements about a boat and the land, so tha
a sentence like the one under consideration would be likel
to stick in the student's mind. Thus, again, Joyce carrie
over in Stephen's thought a memory which is fully unde
standable only in the light of the *Stephen Hero* manu
script—and then only after investigation.

The second Gaelic sentence ('I am a priest'), Stephen, whose monkish mind I have discussed, would find personally applicable, quotation or no quotation.

6—Molly Bloom

[For an explanation of the abbreviations used, see Abbreviations preceding Notes.]

1. Herbert Gorman, *James Joyce* [New York, 1948], p. 281, n. 1. For more on models for Molly, see Richard Ellmann, *James Joyce* (New York, 1959), pp. 353, 386–89.   2. U63.

3. Cf. U64: "The same young eyes." (cchocd, after a Spanish' thought, on p. 375: "*señorita* young eyes"); p. 273: "Big Spanishy eyes."; p. 367: "That's where Molly can knock spots off them. It is the blood of the south. Moorish. Also the form, the figure."; p. 371: "Moorish eyes."; p. 748: "Ive my mothers eyes and figure anyhow he always said" (part of an addition in H).

4. U222.

5. Cf. U273: "Her wavyavyeavyheavyeavyevyevy hair"; p. 375: "black hair".

6. Cf. U91: "Body getting a bit softy. . . . But the shape is there. The shape is there still. Shoulders. Hips. Plump."

7. Cf. U715: "a pair of outsize ladies' drawers of India mull, cut on generous lines,".

8. Cf. U621: "She has the Spanish type. Quite dark, regular brunette, black."

9. U636.   10. U83; W21:7.   11. U365; W105:7.

12. U728–29; W184:5.   13. U740–41; W187:6–7.

14. Frank Budgen, *James Joyce and the Making of ULYSSES* (New York, 1934), p. 266.

15. U730; W184:6.   16. U756; W202:2.

17. U756; W200:2. The present addition and the last one were probably inspired by the "only natural weakness" which precedes them on the same page.

18. U762; W200:7. The present addition is introduced shortly after "it didnt make me blush why should it either

its only nature" (p. 762) and shortly before "after that hed kiss anything unnatural" (*ibid.*).

In W196:8 Joyce adds "as if the one nature gave wasnt enough for anybody" (U753).

19. U725; W182:3.

20. U736; W191:3. U's "any any fool" is an erratum; cf. H, S, OP.

21. U765; W204:8. He deletes the apostrophe in W202:8.

22. U757; W200:3. Then Joyce changes "they havent pocket" to "all their 20 pockets aren't" (for comment, see below, n. 68), and after "them" he adds "even". (He deletes the apostrophe in H.)

I corrects U's "I'll to "Ill". Cf. H, S, OP.

23. U759; W202:4. For an addition made after "not good of me" in W200:5, see text to which n. 60 refers.

24. U727; W184:4. The rest of the text is built up in W185:5.

25. U734; W192:2. He also deletes the apostrophe.

26. U739; W187:5–6. The record of Molly's recent desire is also further testimony regarding her technique. At least once before Molly had given her eyes "that look", with far-reaching consequences. Cf. U173: "Flowers her eyes were, take me, willing eyes."; p. 768: "then I asked him with my eyes to ask again".

27. U758; W201:3. He also deletes the apostrophes.

28. W203:3.   29. U764; W202:7.   30. H.

31. U725; R. Joyce deletes the apostrophe in W184:3.

32. Made available to me by Mr. R. F. Roberts. To be referred to hereafter as Roberts typescript.

33. W184:3. In W185:3 Joyce inserts "Id" before "let".

34. U728; R. In W185:5 he changes "one" to "1" and deletes the apostrophe in "we'll".

35. W182:5.   36. H.   37. U728; W183:5.

38. U730; Roberts typescript.   39. H.

40. U741; W187:7. He also uncapitalizes "Shadow". In H he deletes the apostrophe.

For more of Molly's strategy in winning Bloom, see especially her account of his proposal (U767–68).

41. U755; W201:1.   42. W200:1.

43. H. Joyce added "where he oughtnt to be" between "busy" and "he" in W202:1.

U's omission of "he" between "be" and "never" is an erratum. Cf. H, S, OP.

44. U761; W200:6. Then, after "bit" Joyce adds further "off".

45. U748; R. Following "used to be", he adds, as an afterthought, "there the whole time".

He deletes the apostrophe in W197:4.

46. U749; W195:4.   47. U748; W197:4.

48. U758; W202:3. Originally, the insertion was made after "songs" and read "and her lowneck dress as she cant attract them any other way". Then Joyce moved the addition to its present place after "green dress", changing "and her lowneck dress" to "with the lowneck". As a result, Mrs. M'Coy's wardrobe is reduced to a single unattractive garment—and Molly's derogation is complete.

49. U746; W196:2. Then, before the newly added "she" Joyce inserts "and is quite changed they all do they havent half the character a woman has".

U's "Blackwater" is an erratum. Cf. Roberts typescript, H, S, OP.

50. H.

51. U761; W200:6. Here, also, after "all over him" Joyce adds "till he half faints under me"; after "with our", "2".

52. U715; W165:6. Apparently Joyce overlooked the repetition created by his failure to delete "blue" in the original version before introducing the new text; he makes the deletion in W167:6.

53. U761.   54. U734; R.   55. W191:2.

56. U740; W191:6. He capitalizes "bull" in W190:6.

U's "banderillos" is an erratum; Joyce added "banderilleros" in W187:6.

57. U741; Roberts typescript. Joyce capitalizes "gorgeous" in W190:7.

58. W191:7.   59. U745; W195:2.

60. U759; W200:5. The passage I cite, before the present change, was part of an addition to W202:4 discussed in the text to which n. 23 refers.

For more of Molly's thoughts on clothes, and additions
to them, see text to which nn. 150–55 refer and n. 199, below. Consider also the influence of Molly's interest in
clothes upon her use of metaphor: "not to be always and
ever wearing the same old hat" (p. 725); "off her head
with my castoffs" (p. 758).

61. U723; W183:1. U's "I'll" is an erratum; cf. OP, I.

62. U725; Roberts typescript.

63. W184:3. He also deletes the apostrophe. In W185:3
he deletes the final letter of "sometimes".

64. U727; W184:4. In W185:5 he changes "of" to "off"
(the reading of R and Roberts typescript).

U's "don't" is an erratum; Joyce deleted the apostrophe
in W182:4.

65. U739; H.   66. U766; W212:1.   67. W208:2.

68. U766; W208:2. Another addition to the femininity
of Molly's thought occurs in a context already cited (text
to which n. 22 refers). In the inserted phrase "deceitful
men they havent pocket enough for their lies", Joyce gives
the thought a peculiarly feminine twist by altering "they
havent pocket" to "all their 20 pockets aren't" (U757;
W200:3; he deletes the apostrophe in H).

69. U747.   70. U723; W184:1.   71. H.

72. U726; W179:3. For a later version of this passage,
see text to which n. 196 refers.

73. U727; R.

74. W184:4. After "dozen" he adds "he was in great
singing voice". He supplies "eaten" after "have" in H.

75. U728; R.

76. W179:5. Here, also, after "that" Joyce adds "putting it on thick"; and after "spoils" he restores a manuscript reading (R) by altering "them" (also in Roberts
typescript) to "him". The "and" before "did" is gone in
the typescript.

Joyce deletes the apostrophe in W184:5.

77. W182:5.   78. U736; R.

79. W190:3. Joyce had substituted "this" for "an" in
W187:3. The rest of the text is built up in W191:3 and
W192:3.

Two additions to Molly's insight into sex have been mentioned in other connections: "seduce him I know what boys feel with that down on their cheek" (text to which n. 33 refers) and "with the lowneck as she cant attract them any other way" (text to which n. 48 refers).

80. *U*733; W187:1. He also deletes the comma after "Bn".

81. See [W.] Burdett-Coutts, *The Sick and Wounded in South Africa* (London, etc., 1900).

82. *U*734; W192:1. In H Joyce changes "mad" to "bad".

The historical fever is again introduced, for consistency, when Molly thinks about "Gardner going to South Africa where those Boers killed him". After "him" Joyce inserts "with their war and fever" (*U*747; W197:3).

83. Note also Molly's admiring "Im sure he was brave too" (*U*734; part of an addition in Roberts typescript).

84. *U*747; W194:3. Here, also, after "dead" Joyce adds "off their feet". (For comment, see below, n. 120.) The rest of the text is built up in W196:3 and H.

85. Straightforward military expressions occur frequently in Molly's thought. Her personal idiom reflects military influence on p. 750: "this big barracks of a place".

86. *U*758; W201:3. The phrase "skirt duty" was added in another passage and then eliminated. After Molly's thought "and that dyinglooking one", Joyce inserted "that used to be doing skirt duty along the south circular" (*U*723; W179:1). Subsequently, he replaced "that used to be doing skirt duty along" with "off" (W184:1).

Another contribution to Molly's military expression is "a squad of them [children]" (*U*727), part of an addition in W185:5.

87. *U*149; W47:2. The omission of the period after "Spain" is Joyce's.

88. *U*737; H. *mirada* ='look.'

89. *U*743; W192:8. *pisto* = 'fowl juice for the sick; dish of tomatoes and red pepper'; *madrileno* = 'Madrilenian.'

90. *U*745; W198:2. (*embarazada* = 'pregnant.') In

point of time, this addition precedes the last, as changes
made in W198 are incorporated in W195, which is dated
"17 novembre 1921," whereas W192 is dated "25 novemb
[sic] 1921."

In H, after "him" Joyce adds "he was awfully put out
first".

91. U762; W200:7. (*coronado* = 'cuckolded.') Another
change made here was discussed in the text to which n.
18 refers.

92. U762; W203:6. Molly Englishes a Spanish expression of courtesy and respect, *besar los pies* ('to kiss the
feet').

93. U767–68; W210:2. *Ronda* = 'night patrol.'

94. W211:2. (*posadas* = 'inns.') The rest of the text is
built up in W210:2, W211:2, W212:2, W208:3—chronologically ordered—and H.

95. Stuart Gilbert, *James Joyce's ULYSSES: A Study*
(New York, 1952), p. 390, n. 1. Spanish additions mentioned in other connections are "Majestad" (text to which
n. 114 refers) and "Don Poldo de la Flora" (below, n.
100).

96. U747; W195:3. The guide line from the marginal
addition to its intended place in the text ran through "still
it", and the compositor apparently assumed that Joyce intended a deletion, for W196:3, in which the addition is
incorporated, has lost "still it".

Joyce introduced "carrot"—presumably Molly's conception of the word—as part of an addition in R, and the
spelling is maintained in the Roberts typescript, W194–
99(:3), and H.

S, OP, U: "pearl must," "carat".

97. U755; W204:1. F. B. Dresslar, *Superstition and
Education* (Berkeley, 1907), p. 14, lists three superstitions
concerning bubbles on liquids as a sign of money. Molly
seems to extend the scope of the belief, for Dresslar mentions only tea and coffee.

98. U760; W200:5. Then, after "7th" Joyce adds
"card". In H, "journey" appears with a capital, and after
"yes wait yes" Joyce introduces "hold on"—commented

on in the text of "Stylistic Realism in *Ulysses*" to which n. 158 of that essay refers.

99. *U*761; *W*200:6.

100. *U*763; *W*200:8. Then, after "cards" Joyce adds "this morning hed have something to sigh for". Here, also, he capitalizes "suggester". The rest of the text—which includes "Don Poldo de la Flora", another bit of Spanish— is introduced in H.

For an earlier version of this passage, see text to which n. 178 refers.

101. *U*726; Roberts typescript. Joyce deletes the apostrophe in *W*184:4.

To Molly's mind religion brings luck even as a ring does. See text to which n. 96 refers.

102. *U*726; *W*179:4. On a separate line in the marginal addition, "us" was apparently overlooked by the compositor, for *W*181:4 and *W*182:4, in which the addition is incorporated, lack the word.

103. *U*767; *W*208:3. Further superstition is introduced in Molly's memory of a scene with her daughter, discussed in the text to which nn. 135–36 refer.

104. *U*726; Roberts typescript.   105. *U*758; *W*203:3.

106. *U*761; *W*204:5. He also deletes the apostrophe.

107. *W*200:6. Another addition to Molly's incorrect usage was presented in the discussion of her superstitiousness: "I hope theyre bubbles on it for a wad of money from some fellow". (See text to which n. 97 refers.)

108. *U*670.   109. *U*743; R.

110. *W*187:8. In *W*189:8 the passage reads "your sad bereavement symp=athy I always make that mistake and newphew with yous yous in". Joyce underscores "newphew" and writes a marginal "X". *W*192:8 reads "symphathy", and Joyce substitutes "2" for the first "yous". In H he restores "double" before the remaining "yous".

111. *U*'s "sympathy" (corrected to "symphathy" by I) and "newphew" fail entirely to render the process.

H, S, OP: "symphathy", "newphew".

112. *U*743; R.

113. *W*190:8. The final text is achieved in H.

114. U744; W195:1. (Italics mine.) Then, after "going by with" Joyce adds further "the bell bringing"—commented on in the passage of "Stylistic Realism in *Ulysses*" to which n. 73 of that essay refers. The rest of the text is added in W194:1, W196:1, and H.

115. U751; W194:6.

116. W196:6. This proof reads "skerry's", and Joyce deletes the apostrophe. In H he corrects a corrupt "all's" to "all ls". Unfortunately, the compositor appears to have acted on the "X" deleting " 's" but not on the last part of the marginal notation "X ls".

H, S: "skerrys"; OP, U: "Skerrys".

S, EP, S4, S6, S9, OP, U: "getting all at school".

117. See text to which n. 64 refers.

118. U734; W192:2.   119. U754; W203:1.

120. U754–55; W200:1. He also changes "watch" to "see".

Another addition to Molly's colloquialism is made in a passage already cited: "theyd die down dead" becomes "theyd die down dead off their feet" (see above, n. 84).

121. U737; R. *The English Dialect Dictionary* defines *plouter*, of which *plotter* is a variant, as follows: "2. . . . to trifle, dawdle, linger."

U's "pottering" is an erratum. Cf. text to which n. 187 refers, H, S, OP.

122. U747; W197:3. (Italics mine.) He also deletes the apostrophe and reverses the sequence of "they ever".

P. W. Joyce, *English as We Speak It in Ireland* (London & Dublin, 1910), p. 325, defines *skit* as follows: "to laugh and giggle in a silly way."

For a discussion of the context of the present addition in a later stage, see text to which n. 84 refers.

123. U755; W201:1. The *EDD* defines *scoot* (v.[1]), of which *scout* is a variant, as follows: "1. *v.* To eject liquid forcibly; to squirt."

124. U756; W200:2. P. W. Joyce, p. 336, defines *strap* as follows: "a bold forward girl or woman; the word often conveys a sense slightly leaning towards lightness of character."

125. U765; W208:1. The *EDD* defines *handrunning*

(under *hand* [1. sb.]) thus: "consecutively, continuously, in uninterrupted succession."

Other dialect terms introduced in R follow: U723: "dring"; 724: "babbyface"; 728: "glauming" (as indicated in text to which n. 75 refers); 731: "dreeping"; 734: "scrooching"; 749: "lecking". In the Roberts typescript, the following terms are added: *U*731: "skeezing"; 741: "taittering".

Besides dialect words, Molly employs many dialect locutions: "the day . . . Goodwin called . . . and I just after dinner all flushed and tossed with boiling old stew" (*U*732—"and I" etc. added in Roberts typescript)—regarding this construction (also used on pp. 734 [twice: first passage added in Roberts typescript; second, in R], 737, 740 [twice: second passage added in H], 742 [added in H], 748 [added in R], 752, 767), see P. W. Joyce, pp. 33–35; "sure you cant get on in this world without style" (*U*736)—regarding this construction (also used on pp. 736 [a second example, added in R], 737 [added in R], 740 [added in W187:6], 763), see P. W. Joyce, pp. 338–39; "he never can explain a thing simply the way a body can understand" (*U*738)—regarding Anglo-Irish "the way" ('in order that'), see P. W. Joyce, p. 36.

Two other Hibernicisms added in revision follow: (1) "if we had even a bath itself" (presented in text to which n. 156 refers). Cf. Molly's "if we I buy a pair of brogues itself" (*U*736). Regarding the Anglo-Irish *itself* ('even'), see P. W. Joyce, pp. 36–37. (2) "you couldnt hear your ears" (*U*727; W185:5). Cf. P. W. Joyce, p. 201: "An odd expression:—'You are making such noise that *I can't hear my ears.*'"

126. U725; W182:2. The apostrophe, deleted in W184:2, persists in W185:3, a later galley, and is deleted again in H.

127. U733; R.

128. W187:1. S, U: "there'll"; OP: "therell".

129. U757; W200:3.

130. U742–43; W190:8. He also changes the second "put" to "print".

This passage provides additions to Molly's technique of

attraction beyond those treated in the text to which nn. 31 ff. refer.

131. W192:8. The rest of the text is introduced in H.

Two further additions to Molly's peevishness have been discussed in another connection: "the fat lot" and "Jamesy" (text to which nn. 118–19 refer).

132. U735; W192:2. His intention was evidently misunderstood, as H reads "make that one made them" and Joyce deletes "made them".

He appears to have altered "Sparrows" to "Lewers" between H and publication.

Note that he has also confused Molly's tenses. In H he changes "make" to "made"—still more confusion of tenses.

133. U753; R.   134. W198:7. S, OP, U: "doesnt".

135. W195:7.   136. W196:7.   137. U750; W198:5.

138. U758; W202:3.

139. W200:4. Joyce deletes the apostrophe in "I'll" in W201:3 and W200:4 (chronologically ordered); the apostrophe in "doesn't", in W203:3.   140. H.

141. U730; W182:7. U's "I'll" is an erratum; cf. H, S, OP.   142. W184:7.

143. W185:8. Here, also, after "show" he adds "him"; after "too", "we did it".   144. U748; W198:4.

145. See text to which n. 29 refers.

146. U729–30; W185:7.   147. U735; R.

148. Roberts typescript.   149. W187:2.

150. U736: R.

151. W187:3. He also changes "an" to "this".

152. W191:3.

153. W190:3. Discussed in the text to which n. 79 refers.

154. W192:3. He gets rid of the apostrophes in W188:3, W191:3, and H. In W192:3 he changes "four" to "4" before "years". In H, after "like" he deletes "new".

155. U741; W187:7.

156. U748; W196:4. In H, after "itself" Joyce inserts "or my own room anyway".

157. U754; W196:8.   158. U757; W204:2.

159. W203:2. Here, also, he changes "sixteen" to "16".

160. In the final text, Molly thinks about music constantly. Consider, furthermore, the probable responsibility of "the choirstairs performance" (p. 748) for "the chamber performance" (p. 749), part of an addition discussed in the text to which n. 46 refers.

161. *U*732; Roberts typescript. The sailor had growled "*For England . . . home and beauty*" as he begged. When he "bayed" the last three words towards Molly's window, the "gay sweet chirping whistling within went on a bar or two, ceased." Then followed Molly's contribution (*U*222).

M. J. C. Hodgart and M. P. Worthington, *Song in the Works of James Joyce* (New York, 1959), p. 68, give the title of the sailor's song as *The Death of Nelson*. Words (by S. J. Arnold) and music (by John Braham) are available in Granville Bantock, ed., *One Hundred Songs of England* (Boston, etc. [1914]), pp. 171–75.

162. W184:8. For the added song, which begins with the words "It is a charming girl I love," see J. Benedict, composer, J. Oxenford and Dion Boucicault, librettists, *The Lily of Killarney* (London [1879]), p. 8.

163. *U*744; Roberts typescript. Joyce deletes the apostrophe in W198:1.

The added song is, of course, out of Gilbert and Sullivan's *Mikado*.

164. W195:1. In W196:1 Joyce changes "three" to "3".

165. "O Maritana wildwood flower" (*U*759). This air and the air in the addition under discussion occur in W. V. Wallace's *Maritana*, Act III. The third air—"The Winds that Waft My Sighs to Thee"—also is introduced in proof: see text to which n. 170 refers.

The present addition echoes Bloom's use of the same snatch (*U*506).

166. *U*760; W201:5. He also restores "I" before "ever" (both words were part of an addition in R) and deletes all the apostrophes but that in "I'll". In W203:5 he deletes that one and a persistent other in the first "love's".

167. W203:5. In W200:5, after "Tarifa" Joyce adds "the lighthouse at Europa point".

168. By Clifton Bingham and H. Trotére; in Hugo Frey,

ed., *Robbins Mammoth Collection of World Famous Songs* (Mammoth Series No. 2) (New York [1939]), p. 78. The song is referred to by name in U271, 636, 740, 743. (In the last passage, Molly appears to be derisively adapting part of the refrain, "Time is flying, Love is sighing," to "love is sighing I am dying".)

169. Perhaps he felt that, since Molly had just said "theyre my eyes", the darkness of her eyes (see text to which nn. 9–10 refer) would be sufficient stimulus for her to remember "as darkly bright".

170. U763; W202:7. "The Winds that Waft My Sighs to Thee," by W. V. Wallace, is included in J. C. H., comp., *Good Old Songs We Used to Sing*, II (Boston, etc., 1895), 124–26.

171. U768; W210:2. See text to which n. 93 refers.

In W211:2 Joyce alters "two" to "2"; however, H, S, OP, and U omit "2".

Musical associations added in revision and presented in other connections, follow: (1) "he goes about whistling . . . his huguenots or the frogs march" (text to which n. 159 refers); (2) "Bill Bailey won't you please come home" (text to which n. 199 refers).

172. "The Characterization of Leopold Bloom," *Literature and Psychology*, IX (1959), 3–4.

173. Budgen, p. 264.   174. U671; W174:2.

175. U759; W200:4. Somewhat later, Joyce adds "I dont want to soak it all out of him like the other women do besides he wont spend it" (U766; W211:1). (The final text is achieved in W211:1 and W208:2.)

176. U749; W195:5. In H Joyce deletes "it".

OP, U: "5/-," which was part of an addition in W198:5; but a short hyphen appears to have been mistaken for a period, deleted by Joyce in W195:5.

R, W194–99, H, S: "drove"; S8, OP, U: "drive".

177. See text to which n. 16 refers.

178. U763; W202:7. The "sigh" is of a piece with the introduction in this same galley, just before "so well he may sleep", of "listen to him the winds that waft my sighs to thee" (see text to which n. 170 refers).

The rest of the text is built up in W200:8 (see text to which n. 100 refers, as well as n. 100) and between that galley and H.

179. U723; R.   180. Roberts typescript.

181. W179:1.   182. W185:1.

183. U727–28; W184:5. Joyce supplies the apparently forgotten "me" after "annoyed" in W185:5. The rest of the text is added in W185:5 and between H and publication.

184. U749; W195:4. Here, also, Joyce alters "2" to "4", heightening Molly's grievance at the same time that he adds a reason for affection.

185. U723; W179:1. He deletes the apostrophe in W183:1 and W184:1.

In W184:1, after "much" he adds "a nun".

186. U309: "What's your programme today?"

187. U737; W191:4. He also deletes the apostrophe. U's "pottering" is an erratum; see text to which n. 121 refers.

188. U732; W186 (single page).

189. U735–36; W187:3.

190. W188:3. The inscription in the Darantière stamp in W187 reads:

$$1\text{re}\begin{cases} 18 \text{ octobre } 1921 \\ M^{lle} \text{ Beach} \end{cases}$$

That in W188 reads:

$$2\begin{cases} 3 \text{ novembre } 1921 \\ M^{lle} \text{ Beach} \end{cases}$$

191. U750; R.   192. W194:5.   193. H.

194. U760; W202:5.   195. U766; W210:1.

196. U725–26; W184:3. He also deletes the apostrophe in "wouldn't" and substitutes "the" for the first "his".

A Father Bernard Corrigan is mentioned in U716. Bernard Corrigan, on pp. 631–32 and 689, seems to be a namesake.

U's "couldn't" and "wouldn't" are errata. Joyce deleted the apostrophe in "couldn't" in W179:3.

197. U735; W191:2. Previous allusions to Val Dillon occur in U153, 230, 364, 716.

Note how Molly corroborates our knowledge of the parasitic Lenehan, who gave his version of the ride over Featherbed Mountain on pp. 230–31.

198. H.

199. *U*759; R. He deletes the apostrophe in W201:4. In H, after "home" he adds "her widows weeds wont improve her appearance theyre awfully becoming though if youre goodlooking"—another contribution to Molly's awareness of clothes.

The song "Bill Bailey, Won't You Please Come Home," words and music by Hughie Cannon, is available in J. J. Geller, *Famous Songs and Their Stories* (New York [1931]), pp. 207–10.

200. E. B. Burgum, " 'Ulysses' and the Impasse of Individualism," *Virginia Quarterly Review*, XVII (1941), 563.

7—Stylistic Realism

[For an explanation of the abbreviations used, see Abbreviations preceding Notes.]

1. In "Du Style," *Œuvres complètes de Stendhal* (*Henry Beyle*), p. 311 of vol. (Paris, 1854) which includes "Racine et Shakespeare." For a pertinent commentary, see J. M. Murry, *The Problem of Style* (London, etc., 1925), pp. 78 ff. Especially to our purpose is the following excerpt: "The first thing to remember in examining this definition is that 'thought' (as I have said before) does not really mean 'thought'; it is a general term to cover intuitions, convictions, perceptions, and their accompanying emotions before they have undergone the process of artistic expression or ejection. A man like Stendhal, brought up in the French sensationalist philosophy of the late eighteenth century, lumps them all together under the name of thoughts. . . . The second point is in the phrase, 'the whole effect which the thought ought to produce.' A more truly accurate translation, I think, would be: 'the whole effect which the thought is intended to produce.' At all events, the French hovers between the two meanings."

(p. 79). Murry mistakenly cites Stendhal's definition as from "Racine et Shakespeare."

2. U50; B253, p. 16. 3. U120; W42:4.

4. Cf. U56: "His [Bloom's] hand took his hat from the peg over his initialled heavy overcoat, and his lost property office secondhand waterproof."; p. 60: "His [Bloom's] hand accepted the moist tender gland and slid it into a sidepocket. Then it fetched up three coins from his trousers' pocket and laid them on the rubber prickles."; p. 149: "His [Bloom's] slow feet walked him riverward, reading." In each of these passages, a part of Bloom's body takes on independent activity while his mind is busy elsewhere. In each, the information is conveyed with admirable precision and economy.

5. U249; W69:8.

6. U325–26; W92:6. The rest of the paragraph is built up here in W92, in W91:7, W95:7, and H.

7. U653; W178:3. 8. U372; W106:5.

9. Cf. U180: "In aid of funds for Mercer's hospital." The phrase recurs on p. 251.

10. U472; W137:2.

11. U677; W173:8. Note how "a doll, a boy, a sailor" reproduces the groping process of Bloom's memory as, with increasing individuation, it recalls the discarded toy.

12. U69; W20:2.

13. U94; W34:8. Here, also, after the first sentence, Joyce adds: "Too much John Barleycorn."

14. U108; W25:4.

15. U165; W49:7. Since R reads "laamp", Joyce appears to be restoring text.

16. Cf. *Moore's Irish Melodies, with Symphonies and Accompaniments by Sir John Stevenson* (Boston, 1852), p. 126.

17. U188: "A man of genius makes no mistakes."

18. U30; R. 19. U65; W24:8.

20. U82; W19:1. 21. H.

22. U229; W66:6. In W65:6, after "them" he adds further "for Jervis street."

23. U660–61; W163:2. Here, also, Joyce changes "drank

from" to "substituted"; before "cream" he adds "viscous"; after "occasions" he deletes the question mark and adds "to complete the act begun?" In W175:2, after "Millicent," he adds "(Milly)". The rest of the text was introduced in H.

24. Consider the following:

U651; W177:2:

"Once in 1892 and once in 1893 with Julius Mastiansky, on both occasions in the parlour of his house in Lombard street, west."

After "his" Joyce adds "(Bloom's)".

N.B. The same addition, in the same passage, is made in W178:2. W177 and W178 are identically dated (see below).

U658; W178:8:

"Because of the surety of the sense of touch in his firm full masculine feminine passive active hand.

"What quality did it possess but with what counteracting influence?"

After "it" Joyce adds "(his hand)".

U664; W163:5:

"How many previous encounters proved their preexisting acquaintance?

"Two. The first in the lilacgarden of Matthew Dillon's house. [sic] Medina Villa, Kimmage road, Roundtown, in 1887, in the company of his mother, Stephen being then of the age of 5 and reluctant to give his hand in salutation. The second in the coffeeroom of Breslin's hotel on a rainy Sundy [sic] in the January 1892, in the company of his father and his granduncle, Stephen being then 5 years older."

Before "mother", "father", and "granduncle", Joyce changes "his" to "Stephen's". (Also, after "January" he adds "of".)

U686; W172:6:

"His logical conclusion?" (The preceding question and answer, except for irrelevant differences, read as in U.)

After "His" Joyce adds "(Bloom's)". (The rest of the text is added in W171:6.)

The dates of the galleys containing the above changes (W177 and W178: "15 décembre 1921"; W163: "16 décemb. 1921"; W172: "21 décembre 1921") and the fact that the very galley (W163) in one part of which Joyce fails to clarify his reference, contains just such a clarification in another part, make it perfectly plain that, at the time, his mind dwelt on such improvement. Moreover, Joyce takes pains in this episode as a whole to express his meaning with exaggerated lucidity.

25. U692–93; W170:4. Other lapses follow:
U49–50:
"He lay back at full stretch over the sharp rocks, cramming the scribbled note and pencil into a pocket, his hat tilted down on his eyes. That is Kevin Egan's movement I made nodding for his nap, sabbath sleep. *Et vidit Deus. Et erant valde bona.* Alo! *Bonjour*, welcome as the flowers in May. Under its leaf he watched through peacocktwittering lashes the southing sun."

The excessive distance of "its" from its antecedent is the result of a sequence of associative interpolations. In a manuscript notebook (B253, p. 16), the passage reads: "He stretched backward at full over the sharp boulders, his hat tilted down on his eyes, cramming the scribbled note and pencil into a pocket. Under its leaf he watched through quivering peacock lashes the southing sun." Joyce transfers "his hat tilted down on his eyes" to a position following "pocket.", and between the sentences inserts: "That is Kevin Egan's movement, nodding for his nap. Hlo! *Bonjour*" (The fact that "movement," replaces "gesture." as an afterthought and that "nodding for his nap" is written, with a guide-line, in the margin of p. 17 of the notebook, may explain the need for the repeated addition of the participial phrase in R.)

R reads: "He lay back at full stretch over the sharp rocks, cramming the scribbled note and pencil into a pocket, his hat tilted down on his eyes. That is Kevin Egan's movement I made. Hlo! *Bonjour*. Under its leaf he watched through peacocktwittering lashes the southing sun." After "I made" Joyce adds", nodding for his nap."— and this text, with the addition incorporated and "Hlo" italicized, appears in *The Little Review*, VI (May 1918), 43. (For the process by which "quivering peacock" became "peacocktwittering" in the manuscript notebook, see text to which n. 2 refers.)

H, after a typographical correction, is identical with *U*. *U*218:

"Moored under the trees of Charleville Mall, Father Conmee saw a turfbarge,".

*U*485:

"[Bloom] *turns each foot simultaneously in different directions*,".

26. *U*6.   27. *U*7; W1:3.

28. See esp. text to which nn. 61 ff. refer.

29. *U*20; W6:2. The passage will bear further comment (irrelevant to the point I am making in my text). The galley under discussion reads: "He gazed southward over the bay. Eyes, pale as the sea the wind had freshened, paler, firm and prudent. The seas' ruler, he gazed over the bay, empty save for a sail tacking by the Muglins." After "for" Joyce first adds "the smokeplume far [with deleting lines through it] vague on the bright skyline and". Then, after "smokeplume" he adds "of the mailboat".

First, about the change from "far" to "vague" in the very writing of the addition. A bald statement of distance is transformed into a statement not only of distance but also of its effect (as well as that of the brightness of the skyline) upon the appearance of the smokeplume *as Haines sees it*.

And now about the tardily inserted "of the mailboat". Apparently, Joyce, himself clearly visualizing his scene with the recently introduced mailboat in it, first proceeded directly to the smokeplume, and only later, realizing that his reader would expect to be supplied with the source of the smokeplume, added "of the mailboat" for clarification.

A further improvement occurs in H, where Joyce (besides correcting a compositor's error in the placing of the phrase "of the mailboat") eliminates the repetition of 'gazed over the bay', retaining only the one distinctive word in the two expressions about the gazing, namely, "southward": "Eyes, pale as the sea the wind had freshened, paler, firm and prudent. The seas' ruler, he gazed southward over the bay, empty save for the smokeplume of the mailboat, vague on the bright skyline, and a sail tacking by the Muglins."

30. U337; W98:7. 31. U448; W118:1.

32. U484; W140:1. And before "Embrace" he adds "(in nursetender's gown)".

Bloom has thought about Mrs. Thornton twice before (U66, 159).

33. U485; W140:2.

In W133:8 (U487–88), another characteristic speech by Brother Buzz, with appropriate action, is introduced. The proof reads:
"Nip the first rattler.

(*Lieutenant Myers of the Dublin Fire Brigade by general request sets fire to Bloom. Lamentations.*)"
After "rattler" Joyce adds:
                    "BROTHER BUZZ
(invests Bloom in a yellow habit with painted flames and high pointed hat. He places a bag of gunpowder round his neck and hands him over to the civil power, saying) Forgive him his trespasses."
Then, after "with" Joyce adds further "embroidery of".
(The rest of the text must have been introduced between W133 and H. For comment, see text to which n. 110 refers, as well as n. 110.)

34. U82.

35. U486; W140:2. And before "What" he adds "(in bushranger's kit)".

Crab was a character in Mulligan's *national immorality in three orgasms* (U214).

36. U553–54; W129:6. The rest of the text must have been introduced between W129 and H, in which the final version is achieved. [R for this passage begins: "(The widow Dignam, her snubnose and cheeks flushed with deathtalk, tears and Tunny's tawny sherry,". H, like W129:6: "*fears*". R's "tears" and OP's and U's "*tears*" follow B259, n.p., in which Joyce introduced the phrase

"her face flushed with talk, tears & old tawny sherry,".]

The reintroduction of Mrs. Thornton, Brother Buzz, Crab, and Mrs. Dignam helps knit *Ulysses* together.

37. U661; W163:2. The rest of the text was introduced in H.

38. This interpretation is supported by Joyce's constant emphasis in the penultimate episode upon complete explicitness.

39. U152.

40. The kinds of success listed reflect the various aspects of Bloom's all-round failure.

41. U669; W174:1. Bloom's interest in moral apothegms does not manifest itself for the first time in the present addition. Early in the morning Bloom considered: "Might manage a sketch. By Mr and Mrs L. M. Bloom. Invent a story for some proverb which?" (U69). In the hospital scene he was taken to task for dispensing "apothegms of dubious taste to restore to health a generation of unfledged profligates" (p. 403; "apothegms of dubious taste" is part of an addition in H). And dominating these details, there is Bloom's triteness, which leans heavily on moral apothegms.

On the first of the newly introduced titles, Joyce composed during his own schoolyears, choosing Ulysses for his subject. (Valery Larbaud, "James Joyce," *La Nouvelle revue française*, April 1, 1922, pp. 404–5; Herbert Gorman, *James Joyce* [New York, 1948], p. 45.) This experience is utilized once more in *Finnegans Wake*, p. 306: "Your Favorite Hero or Heroine".

42. U164; W49:6.   43. U361; W105:4.

44. U365; W104:7. Here, also, after "Where" Joyce adds "do".

45. W105:7. Joyce first wrote "to show her calves", then replaced "calves" with "understandings", a slang term which is peculiarly suited to Bloom, considering his love of 'adaptations.'

In W105:7, also, after "there." Joyce gives Bloom an insight: "Longing to get the fright of their lives."

46. U732; W183:8. OP, U: "Dolphins", "couldnt".

47. U746; W198:2. In W194:2, Joyce changes "Albertis" to "Benady Bros".

48. "I wanted to fire his pistol" (U746).

49. U749; W197:4.

50. W198:4. In W195:4, after "mutton" Joyce adds "the very name is enough".

51. H.   52. U152, 169.

53. U668; R.   54. W163:8.

55. In the context of the passage under discussion, Bloom recalls verbatim the advertisement (or that part of it?) which he saw in the morning (cf. U73–74): "What is home without Plumtree's Potted Meat?" etc.

56. W175:8.

57. The question-and-answer unit in which the passage under discussion occurs, the preceding two units, and part of the third answer back, all render indirectly Bloom's "cogitations" on the "art of advertisement" (U667).

For an earlier performance of Bloom's at anagrams, see U662.

58. U70; W20:4.   59. U76; W21:2.

60. U94; W33:8.

61. U59; W24:2. The whole addition follows: into a blank space of four lines between "by George." (end of paragraph) and "The model farm" (beginning of next paragraph), Joyce writes:
"The way her crooked skirt swings at each whack.

"The ferretcycd porkbutcher folded the sausages he had snipped off with blotchy fingers, sausagepink. [Note the splendid picture here added.] Sound meat there like a stallfed heifer."
Then, at the bottom of the page, Joyce inserts a new opening for the next paragraph: "He took up a page from the pile of cut sheets [sic]". "He", which seems to refer to the "porkbutcher", actually, and awkwardly, refers to Bloom. The sentence is apparently added to make clear the source of the following speculations, by Bloom, on the model farm.

From here on, I am lumping together all changes, whether made by the author as such or through the minds of his characters. I have already shown that Joyce himself does not make the distinction.

62. U_{59}. 63. U_{275}.

64. U_{165}; W_{50}:7. 65. U_{189}; W_{55}:5.

66. U_{337}; W_{97}:7.

67. U_{486}; W_{140}:2. It is in the context of this passage that Joyce also introduces the pictorial "bushranger's kit" presented above, n. 35. A similar addition in the interest of picture-making is that of the "nursetender's gown", presented above, n. 32.

68. U_{510}; W_{124}:3.

69. U_{688}; W_{172}:8, continued in W_{169}:1.

70. U_{736}; W_{188}:3. 71. U_{85}; W_{19}:3.

72. Bloom has just thought: "Enjoy a bath now . . . the gentle tepid stream." (U_{85}). His interest in warmth also figures in one of the imagined recreations of "Flowerville": "discussion in tepid security of unsolved historical and criminal problems:" (p. 700).

73. U_{744}; W_{195}:1. Additions of vivid detail discussed in other connections follow: the change of "far" to "vague" (see above, n. 29), and the insertion of "across his stained square of newspaper" (see below, n. 106).

74. U_{206-7}.

75. Evidently Joyce's characters share some of his predilections. Harry Levin has remarked on their "preoccupation with language." (*James Joyce: A Critical Introduction* [Norfolk, Connecticut (1941)], p. 126.)

76. U_{46}; W_{10}:6. Here Joyce also changes the second period to an exclamation mark.

77. U_{70}; W_{20}:4. U's comma after the second "da" is an erratum; cf. S, OP.

78. U_{81}; W_{21}:6. In W_{36} (single page) before "Punish" Joyce adds further "Penance.", which clarifies the shift in Bloom's thought from "Then I will tell you all." to "Punish me, please.", and balances off against "Confession." as an introductory thought.

It should be noted that only "Punish me, please." is an unquestionable dramatization. "Then I will tell you all.", which echoes the letter from Martha Clifford (U_{77}), may be regarded as drama only if we assume that Bloom is not merely recalling Martha's sentence as an instance of the desire to confess but that he is dramatizing confession and putting the sentence into the mouth of the confessor. We may presume that he is dramatizing confession since, in the next sentence, in the same addition, he dramatizes penance; and the adaptation would be typical of Bloom.

Bloom recalls Martha's sentence once more at twilight (U366).

79. U81–82; W36.

80. "And I schschschschschsch. And did you chacha-chachacha? And why did you?" (U81)

81. U82; W21:6. The whole addition includes, as ending: "Monasteries and convents."

82. U82; W21:7. The period at the end of the addition is Joyce's—a mistake which he apparently failed to catch. Cf. S, OP, *U*.

83. "Excuse, miss, there's a (whh!) just a (whh!) fluff." (U82)

84. U154; W47:7.

85. U159; W49:3. The addition is so placed that it may be mistaken as coming between "Not stillborn of course." and "They are not even registered and Y.M.C.A." (U159 —in W50:3, Joyce deletes "and Y.M. C.A."). The printer made this mistake in setting up W50. In H, Joyce rearranged the text as he had originally intended it.

H, S, OP, *U*: "nyumyum". In W50:3 Joyce clearly corrected a misprint to "nyumnyum".

86. "Well, God is good, sir." (U66)

87. See text to which n. 32 refers.

88. U180; W53:4. Here, also, Joyce alters "wine" to "stuff", a demotion appropriate to the context of Bloom's thought, as witness the addition, also made here, after "drank.", of "Vintage wine for them, the year marked on a dusty bottle." In W54:4 Joyce alters "assizer" to "assizes".

89. U213–14; W61:4. The whole addition includes, as ending, the independent paragraph: "He stopped at the stairfoot." Between W62, a later galley containing this passage, and H, Joyce must have inserted "mopping," before "chanting".

In W61 Joyce is evidently rectifying a printer's error,

for both R and *The Little Review*, VI (May 1919), 34,
contain the text added, except that Buck Mulligan's
speech consists of one sentence: "—The most beautiful
book that has come out of Ireland in my time." This version follows more closely than does the final text ("out of
our country") Yeats's preface to Lady Gregory's *Cuchu-
lain of Muirthemne* (London, 1902), p. vii: "I think this
book is the best that has come out of Ireland in my time."
Joyce may have changed "Ireland" to "our country" in
order to point up Yeats's nationalism, but a later echo of
the same passage in Yeats retains the original word: "Most
beautiful book come out of Ireland in my time." (U417.
This sentence occurs as early as R.)

The addition of "One thinks of Homer." in W61 may
glance at both Yeats and George Moore, for Moore, in his
introduction to Edward Martyn's *"The Heather Field"
and "Maeve"* (London, 1899), p. xx, called Yeats's *The
Countess Cathleen* "a play, beautiful as anything in
Maeterlinck, a play possessing all the beauties of the Prin-
cess Maleine, and the beauty of verses equal to the verses
of Homer." [Joyce had attended the double première of
The Countess Cathleen and *The Heather Field* in 1899;
in 1919, in Zurich, he recommended that the English
Players produce *The Heather Field*. See Gorman, p. 60;
Richard Ellmann, *James Joyce* (New York, 1959), pp. 68–
69, 468.]

It may be noted that in W61:3 Joyce added, in another
mocking speech of Mulligan's: "Our players are creating
a new art for Europe like the Greeks or M. Maeterlinck."
(U213) Cf. Gorman, p. 136, quoting Joyce: " 'Synge's
play is Greek,' said Yeats, etc."

90. U314; W86:4. Here, also, after "son" Joyce adds
"off Island bridge".

U's "Government" is an erratum. Cf. R, S, OP.

91. U366; W104:8. Here, also, after "when" Joyce fills
in the postern scene with "they hold him out to do".

M. J. C. Hodgart and M. P. Worthington, *Song in the
Works of James Joyce* (New York, 1959), pp. 75, 191,
identify the phrase "Papa's pants will soon fit Willie" with

the American nonsense song *Looking through the Knothole*.

92. U366–67; W104:8. In H Joyce eliminates the repetition of "night" by altering "all night" to "in the dark".

93. U66; W22:8.

94. "He [Bloom] stood by the nextdoor girl at the counter. *Would* she buy it too, calling the items from a slip [in (see I, S, OP)] her hand. Chapped: washing soda." (*U*59; italics mine.)

95. Discussed above in "James Joyce: A Study in Words."

96. U42; B253, p. 8.   97. W10:2.

98. U50; B253, p. 17. R, W7:4, H: "waters" and "widely flowing". W7:4 and H, like *U*, have no comma before "oos", and have a colon before "bounded".

Besides onomatopoeia, observe also Joyce's marvellous use of rhythms, to be treated in the text to which nn. 124 ff. refer.

99. U86; W34:1. Cf. p. 571: *"woman's slipperslappers"*; also, p. 466: "Mother Slipperslapper" (a variant—developed in W119:8 from "Mother Slipperslopper", presumably to form an echoing pattern with the other passages—on "old Mother Slipper-Slopper"; cf. Eric Partridge, *A Dictionary of Slang and Unconventional English* [New York, 1937], p. 783).

100. U96; W32:2. He does not touch "out". OP, *U*: "Out".

101. U112; W26:6. OP, *U*: "greatgrandfather Kraahraark!", "awfullygladaseeragain", "amarawf", "kopthsth".

102. U112; W25:6.

103. U132; W43:6. The rest of the speech, which is typical of Lenehan, must have been introduced between this galley and H.

104. U434; R.   105. U167; W51:1.

106. U167; W51:1. I have supplied the first "un" from W52:1, which incorporates the addition here made. In W51:1, there is a gap between "hum" and "thu", part of the page, in a folded corner of the proof sheet, being torn out. S, OP, *U*: "hum un thu".

In W52, after "you" Joyce adds ", faith". He completed the picture (with "across his stained square of newspaper") in H.

107. Frank Budgen, *James Joyce and the Making of ULYSSES* (New York, 1934), p. 52. The passage which Joyce read occurs in U45. (S, OP, U: "gigant".)

108. U335; W97:5. Here, also, after "Alf" Joyce adds "round him like a leprechaun". The rest of the text must have been added between this galley and H.

109. See above, n. 33.

110. U487. We are now prepared for the appearance of Lieutenant Myers of the Dublin Fire Brigade who, shortly afterward, sets fire to Bloom (p. 488).

The brigade spoke at the close of the preceding episode: "Pflaap! Pflaap! . . . Pflaap! . . . Pflaaaap! . . . Pflaap! . . . Pflaaaap!" (pp. 420–21). And it appears twice again (pp. 427, 471 [added in W135:1]) before its speech is reintroduced.

111. U508; W124:2. OP, U: "He", "butt."

112. U578; W132:4. Before the speech Joyce has the following instruction: "vers /".

H, OP, U: "ho rhother's hest.", "*cobblestones*". H, OP, I (correcting U's "*clothes to*"): "*clothes on to*".

The division into "ho rhother's" seems to introduce a desperate gasping attempt to get out the last words in what otherwise might appear to be, under the circumstances, too regular an utterance.

In H, before "*A violent erection*" Joyce inserts "*He gives up the ghost.*" The rest of the text must have been introduced between this proof and publication. The leaping assistants echo p. 299: "there's two fellows waiting below to pull his heels down when he gets the drop and choke him properly" (part of an addition in W84:1).

113. Cf. U279: "Once by the churchyard he had passed and for his mother's rest he had not prayed."

114. "The Croppy Boy," by Carroll Malone, in M. J. Brown, *Historical Ballad Poetry of Ireland* (Dublin and Belfast, 1912), pp. 212–13.

115. E. R. Curtius, *James Joyce und sein Ulysses* (Zürich, 1929), pp. 57–58.

116. U210; W61:1. *U* omits the opening dash. Cf. S, OP.

117. H. *U*'s "Buck" is corrected by I. Cf. also S, OP.

The final form of Buck's name in this passage may owe something to the similar-sounding variation to "Puck" which occurs twice shortly afterward (pp. 212, 213).

Other variations on Malachi ("Buck") Mulligan's name are "Monk Mulligan" (p. 203), "Sonmulligan" (p. 205), and *"Ballocky Mulligan"* (p. 214).

118. U213; W61:2. Eglinton's chin is also satirized in one of 'Puck's' verses: *"Magee that had the chinless mouth."* (p. 213).

"John Eglinton" is the pseudonym of the essayist William Kirkpatrick Magee. Other variations on his names follow: "littlejohn Eglinton" (p. 192), "John sturdy Eglinton" (p. 200), "Second Eglinton" (p. 201; "Second" replaces "John" in H), *"Eglintonus Chronolologos"* (p. 204; *"Eglintonus"* replaces "Eglington" [sic] in W59:3), "MAGEEGLINJOHN" (p. 206; cf. below, n. 181), "Judge Eglinton" (p. 209), "Eglinton Johannes" (p. 211), "John Eclecticon" (*ibid.*; cf. text to which n. 181 refers) and "Tanderagee" (p. 499).

119. U432; W116:3.

120. (U47)—and *biscuit* to "biscuitfully" (p. 122), as also the adjective *alive* to the noun "alive" (p. 112).

121. U557–58; W130:2. The whole addition includes, after the sentence I have cited, the following: *"Ward Union huntsmen and huntswomen live with them, hot for a kill. From Six Mile Point, Flathouse, Nine Mile Stone follow the footpeople with knotty sticks, hayforks, salmongaffs, lassos, bearbaiters with tomtoms, toreadors with bullswords, grey negroes waving torches."* Then, after *"pack"* Joyce adds further *"of staghounds"*; after *"follows"*, *", nose to the ground,"*; after *"lassos,"*, *", flockmasters with stockwhips,"*.

Here, also, he changes the opening *"The"* to "A stout"; after *"fox"* he adds *", drawn from covert,"*; after *"pointed,"*, *",having buried his grandmother,"*; after *"swift"*, *"for the open"*; after *"brighteyed"*, *",seeking badger earth,"*.

The Ward Union huntsmen and huntswomen hot for a kill, and the staghounds, echo Bloom's earlier thought: "Lady Mountcashel has quite recovered after her confinement and rode out with the Ward Union staghounds at the enlargement yesterday at Rathoath. Uneatable fox. . . . Weightcarrying huntress. . . . First to the meet and in at the death." (p. 158). (In proof, Lady Mountcashel "rode out with the Meath hounds." The final version is introduced in W49:2.)

The fox's disposition of his grandmother echoes the riddle which Stephen put to his class in the morning and solved thus: "—The fox burying his grandmother under a hollybush." (pp. 27–28) The riddle recurs, with a significant variation, in the brothel scene (p. 544), not very long before the reintroduction of the solution.

Note the completeness of the picture which Joyce has built up from so meagre a beginning.

The final version (except for typographical details) must have been worked out between W130 and H.

122. U252. For analogues, cf. *clip-a-clap* and *clip-clop*.

123. U561. The coinage took place between B259, n.p. ("claps") and R ("clipclaps").

124. Budgen, pp. 19–20. The sentences discussed occur in U166. In R, they read: "Perfumes of embraces assailed him. His hungered flesh obscurely, mutely craved to adore."

125. U166–67; W51:1.   126. U85.

127. U189. Joyce had already made use of the first half of this word when a door "whispered: ee: cree." (p. 116). The form of the whole word might have come to him from the OED entry "Cree, crie" (= 'create'). Should evidence of Joyce's acquaintance with the OED be necessary, see below, n. 161.

128. U252.   129. U271.   130. U561.   131. U256.

132. U439.

133. U461. For analogues, cf. *jig-a-jig, jig-a-jog, jig-jig, jig-jog,* and *jog-jog.*

134. U524.

135. U562. Concerning Joyce's later partiality for re-

duplicates, see T. P. Beyer, "A Note on the Diction of *Finnegans Wake*," *College English*, II (December 1940), 275–77.

136. U68–69; W20:2. Other specimens of this technique follow: "Excuse, miss, there's a (whh!) just a (whh!) fluff." (p. 82); "Sllt. The nethermost deck of the first machine jogged forward its flyboard with sllt the first batch of quirefolded papers." (etc.—p. 120); "All flushed (O!), panting, sweating (O!), all breathless. . . . And flushed yet more (you horrid!), more goldenly." (p. 256); "Shebronze, dealing from her jar thick syrupy liquor for his lips, looked as it flowed (flower in his coat: who gave him?), and syrupped with her voice: . . . Miss Kennedy passed their way (flower, wonder who gave), bearing away teatray." (p. 261); "So I just went round to the back of the yard to pumpship and begob (hundred shillings to five) while I was letting off my (*Throwaway* twenty to) letting off my load" (etc.—p. 329); "Kiss and delighted to, kiss, to see you." (p. 362); "Mr Bloom inserted his nose. Hm. Into the. Hm. Opening of his waistcoat." (p. 369)

137. U197; W57:5.   138. W58:5.

139. U237; R.

140. W67:5. W68, incorporating this change, omits the first "in their saddles", as do S, OP, and *U*.

U's "Pembrook" is corrected by I. Cf. also S, OP.

141. U244.

142. U522; W125:5–6. Then, after "up!" Joyce adds: "A cockhorse to Banbury cross."; and he alters *"ridehorse"* to *"cockhorse"*.

OP and U omit "in the,"; S, EP, S4, S6 do not.

143. U558; R.

144. H. This is also the reading in B259, n.p.

145. U730–31; W182:7. Joyce appears to be restoring the prancing rhythm, for in typescript (made available to me by Mr. R. F. Roberts) he altered "anything for an excuse to put his hand near my drawers drawers all the time" to "anything for an excuse to put his hand anear me drawers all the time". (He eliminates the apostrophes

and period in W184:7, and changes "all the time" to "the whole blessed time" in W185:8.)

The rhythm of insistence was employed at one stage in the composition of the Gerty MacDowell episode: "But Tommy said he wanted the ball and Edy told him no that baby was playing with the ball and if he took it there'd be wigs on the green but Tommy said it was his ball and he wanted his ball his ball and he pranced on the ground, if you please." (U346). In H, Joyce, for reasons best known to himself, eliminated the prancing repetition by deleting the second half of "his ball his ball", thereby restoring, for this phrase, the reading in B257 (p. 8) and R.

146. U262; W73:7. The conclusion of the sentence, in R, reads: "she said."

147. U263; W73:7. 148. U265; W76:2.

149. A "base barreltone" according to Molly (U759). Through Bloom's thought (p. 152) we learn that Molly has used the expression before. It occurs to Bloom thrice again during the day (pp. 266, 278, 510).

150. U266; W76:2. 151. U491.

152. U504.

153. U506; W123:7. When the moth's speech was added in B259 (opposite p. 12), the first line read: "I'm a tiny tiny thing,". In R, this version is incorporated in the text.

154. U688–89; W170:1. The whole addition includes, after the question and answer I have cited, the two units of question and answer which occur next in the final version. There is one variation between Joyce's addition and the final text: Joyce wrote "Ned Lambert (in bed), Tom Kernan (in bed),".

155. Since "Saint" is here used as a prefix, its vowel is unstressed.

156. U714–15; W167:6. OP, U: "by the hypothesis".

157. U760; W201:4. 158. H.

159. W200:5. Note also the groping questions in the context: "what was the seventh card after that" (likewise added in W200), "didn't I dream something too".

Uncertainty moves with a different step through Molly's

"wait O Jesus wait yes that thing has come on me yes" (p. 754).

160. Most of the exceptions occur, understandably, in Joyce's attempts to verbalize various sounds. See text to which nn. 95 ff. refer.

161. Cf. Frank Budgen, "James Joyce," *Horizon*, III (February 1941), 107–8: "In my hearing he [Joyce] answered (perhaps for the hundredth time) the question: 'Aren't there enough words for you in the five hundred thousand of the English language?' 'Yes, there are enough of them, but they are not the right ones.'"

Cf. also Budgen, "Joyce's Chapters of Going Forth by Day," *ibid.*, IV (September 1941), 177: "I have already quoted a saying of Joyce's (evidently a practised hand-off for a straight tackler), 'Yes, there are enough words in the Oxford Dictionary, but they are not the right ones.'"

162. U8; W2:4. 163. *OED*.

164. See text to which n. 148 refers.

165. U269. In *Finnegans Wake*, Joyce elaborates *lovesoft* into "lovesoftfun" (p. 607), to pun upon *lots of fun*.

166. U375; W107:8.

167. H. And "dirty girl" becomes "dirty bracegirdle". In other words, Joyce probably borrowed "girl" for "girlwhite" from "dirty girl", while with "dirty girl" he conflated the memory of "Mrs Bracegirdle" (p. 363), who was herself introduced between W105:6 and H.

For "girlwhite" there are, of course, analogous *-white* compounds, of which Joyce uses the following: "lilywhite" (p. 675), "milkwhite" (pp. 55, 335, 471), and "saltwhite" (pp. 50, 113).

168. U258. In *Finnegans Wake* he produces "girlglee" (p. 182) and "girlsfuss" (p. 430).

169. U446; W117:7. Cf. *Finnegans Wake*, p. 299, n. 2: "scumhead."

170. U687; W171:8. Cf. "nothandle" (U64; introduced as two words in W24:7, the addition appears as one word in W22:6 and H) and the history of the already current "notwithstanding" (used on pp. 634, 655). Cf. also *Finnegans Wake*, p. 161: "nothave" and "nothalf"; p. 175:

"Notpossible"; p. 455: "Notshall"; and, on p. 124: "butnot".

171. H. (Here Joyce also added "reciprocal" before "flesh".) Cf. *Finnegans Wake*, p. 442: "ournhisn"; p. 446: "ouryour".

172. U689; W170:1. The whole addition includes the answer to this question. This answer is obviously modelled on that to the third question back, likewise added here (as pointed out above, n. 154).

For the chiming of the bells, also introduced here, see text to which nn. 154–55 refer.

173. See text to which n. 120 refers, as well as n. 120.

174. U125; W42:8. Here, also, before the last "his" Joyce adds "raking".

175. *OED.*   176. U513.

177. *Ibid.* A similar piece of agglutination and conversion is "Sherlockholmesing" (p. 620), which antedates and differs from the only specimen given by the *OED* (*Supplement*) for the use of the full name as a verb.

Cf. *Finnegans Wake*, p. 121: "blackartful"; p. 122: "toomuchness" (cf. *OED s.v.* "Too," 6.a.) and "fartoomanyness"; p. 184: "noondayterrorised"; p. 199: "hungerstriking"; p. 513: "inandouting".

178. U662–63; W163:4, W175:4, and H. W163 bears the following inscription:

$$1 \begin{cases} \text{16 décemb. 1921} \\ \text{M}^\text{lle}\text{ Beach} \end{cases}$$

W175 bears the following inscription:

$$2 \begin{cases} \text{30 décembre 1921} \\ \text{M}^\text{lle}\text{ Beach} \end{cases}$$

179. Louise Pound, *Blends, Their Relation to English Word Formation* (Heidelberg, 1914), p. 2.

180. See text to which n. 106 refers. And cf. *Finnegans Wake*, p. 164: "so munch to the cud" (in a context involving "stomach" and "digesting"—p. 163); p. 317: "munchantman".

181. U211; W61:2. In H, before his statement "Names! What's in a name?" (U206) "JOHN EGLINTON" becomes "MAGEEGLINJOHN", a blend of *Magee* (his real name), *Eglinton,* and *John*.

182. See text to which n. 118 refers. Eglinton is joined, in *Finnegans Wake* (p. 81), by Napoleon and Wellington as "Nippoluono" and "Wei-Ling-Taou."

183. U504; W123:6.

184. S, OP, U. R, OP, U: "female"; but Joyce changed "female" to "fumale" in the typescript (now at the Lockwood Memorial Library of the University of Buffalo), hence S, EP, S4, S6, S9: "fumale". For other puns on *female*, cf. *Finnegans Wake*, p. 437: "femurl"; p. 539: "fimmel"; p. 564: "femecovert"; p. 617: "Femelles". For other puns on *fume*, cf. *ibid.*, p. 219: "perfumance"; p. 320: "blastfumed"; p. 333: "mewseyfume"; p. 413: "fumiform"; p. 624: "parafume".

185. U591–92; W143:6–7.

186. S, S4, OP, U: *"with their tooraloolooloolooloo lay."*

187. See text to which n. 136 refers, as well as n. 136.

188. U70 (in Bloom's memory), 588.

189. U104: "With your tooraloom tooraloom."

190. U481.

191. The coincidence occurred once before in a passage dealing with Corny Kelleher:

"Corny Kelleher fell into step at their side.

"—Everything went off A I, he said. What?

"He looked on them from his drawling eye. Policeman's shoulders. With your *tooraloom tooraloom.*

"—As it should be, Mr Kernan said.

"—What? Eh? Corny Kelleher said.

"Mr Kernan *assured* him." (U104. Italics mine.) Joyce, who knit together *Ulysses* with preternatural care, surely bore in mind, if he did not return to, this preceding passage relating to Kelleher, when Kelleher reappeared in nighttown. Thus there would be operating in Joyce's brain two coincidences of -*sure*- and *tooraloom.*

192. U70, 481, 588. On p. 70 (as indicated above, n. 188) Bloom remembers Kelleher's singing of the snatch; on p. 481 (as indicated above, n. 190) Bloom sings it on his own; on p. 588 Kelleher himself sings it.

The punctuation I have given is that of pp. 481, 588; that of p. 70 includes commas in the series of repeating words. The divergence occurs in S and OP, also.

193. U70. This same "tay" no doubt accounts for the last syllable in "reassuraloomtay".

194. U666; W163:7. Here, also, after "first arts" Joyce adds "second arts"; after "courses of" he adds "the royal", at the same time uncapitalizing "University".

195. U516: "Nes. Yo." For other transpositions, cf. text to which n. 56 refers, and *Finnegans Wake*, p. 16: "oach eather"; p. 106: "*Inglo-Andean*"; p. 144: "Jolio and Romeune"; p. 189: "wious pish"; p. 349: "pughs and keaoghs"; p. 460: "stuesser . . . Vanilla"; p. 569: "Nowno and . . . Brolano".

196. H.   197. Levin, p. 168, quoting U141.